Ch

C000056790

Pocket party phrasebook

Flirt, drink and be merry in ten languages

Chambers

First published by Chambers Harrap Publishers Ltd 2007
7 Hopetoun Crescent
Edinburgh EH7 4AY

ISBN: 978 0550 10392 5

Contributors

Teresa Alvarez
Pauline Gaberel
Allan Christian Hansen
Mike Harland
Mara Kuijpers
Evy Markopoulou
Lalita Markopoulou
Debora Mazza
Cristina Mendes
Kate Nicholson

Lena Nordman
Georges Pilard
Robert Porter
Natasja Reslow
Orlanda Ward
Donald Watt
Jörg Weber
Daniel Williams
Jakub Žytek

Editor & Project Manager
Kate Nicholson

Publishing Manager
Anna Stevenson

Prepress
Nicolas Echallier

Designed and typeset by Chambers Harrap Publishers Ltd, Edinburgh
Printed and bound by Thomson Litho, East Kilbride, Scotland.
Illustrations by Art Explosion

Contents

Introduction

This brand new multilingual phrasebook from Chambers has been specially written for young (and young-at-heart) travellers who want to experience authentic European nightlife along with the locals. Covering ten popular European languages, it's packed with essential phrases for a great night out (plus a few for the morning after!), whether you're relaxing in the pub or dancing till dawn.

The *Bare Essentials* chapter provides a concise introduction to each language, giving some basic phrases and explaining the easy-to-use phonetic transcription system: just follow the simple guidelines to make yourself understood wherever you're heading.

The seven thematic chapters take you from planning your evening to keeping safe, and cover topics including bars, clubs, parties and culture. You'll find every English word and phrase translated into all ten languages, each followed by its phonetic transcription. Each chapter opens with a few key terms, and the phrases are helpfully divided into those you're more likely to hear ('Listen up!' sections) and those you might want to use yourself ('Over to you').

Each chapter includes a wealth of practical and cultural information on the social scene in the various countries, to help you fit in with the locals and avoid tourist blunders. And look out for the 'Fun facts' dotted throughout the text, providing nuggets of local information you might not find in a guidebook. Finally, we've included a cheesy chat-up line for every situation, so you need never be tongue-tied on holiday again!

If you're tired of the typical tourist haunts and want to know what the locals get up to at night, then this book is for you. Slip it in your pocket and get ready for a night to remember!

Bare Essentials

This section includes pronunciation tips for each language as well as a few key words and phrases to get you started.

Every foreign-language phrase in this book is followed by a phonetic transcription in *italics*. The following pages explain the transcription system used for each language: by following these simple guidelines you will be able to make yourself understood. Words have been broken down into syllables: note that in each case you should stress the one(s) shown in **bold**.

In this book we have occasionally used the abbreviations *m* (masculine) and *f* (feminine).

Czech

Czech pronunciation is relatively easy once you have mastered a few simple rules, as words are spelled phonetically. Note that the stress always falls on the first syllable of the word (or on any preceding prepostion containing a vowel, eg ***hos**-po-da* pub; *do **hos**-po-dy* (in)to the pub).

Alphabet and pronunciation

The letters of the Czech alphabet are pronounced as follows:

a *a*	**e** *e*	**i** *myek-<u>kee</u> <u>ee</u>*
á *dlo-oo-<u>hee</u> <u>a</u>*	**é** *dlo-oo-<u>hee</u> <u>e</u>*	**í** *dlo-oo-<u>hee</u> myek-*
b *be*	**ě** *ye*	*<u>kee</u> <u>ee</u>*
c *tse*	**f** *ef*	**j** *ye*
č *che*	**g** *ge*	**k** *ka*
d *de*	**h** *ha*	**l** *el*
d' *dye*	**ch** *kha*	**m** *em*

n *en*	**s** *es*	**x** *eeks*
ň *e*	**š** *esh*	**y** *eep-seel-on/*
o *o*	**t** *te*	***tvr**-d<u>ee</u> ee*
ó *dlo-oo-hee <u>o</u>*	**ť** *tye*	**ý** *dlo-oo-<u>hee</u> eep-*
p *pe*	**u** *oo*	*see-lon/ **dlo-oo-***
k *kve*	**ú/ů** *dlo-oo-<u>hee</u> <u>oo</u>*	*<u>hee</u> **tvr**-d<u>ee</u> ee*
r *er*	**v** *ve*	**z** *zed*
ř *erzh*	**w** *dvoy-ee-t<u>e</u> ve*	**ž** *zhed*

Note the following transcriptions used in this book for Czech vowels. Vowels marked with an acute accent are 'long': they are pronounced the same as non-accented ones but are held for approximately twice as long. This is shown by underlining:

a	*a*, like *u* in 'but'
á	<u>*aa*</u>, a long *a* as in 'bar'
e	*e*, a short *e* as in 'get'
é	<u>*e*</u>, like *e* in 'get' but longer
ě	*ye* as in 'yes'
i	*ee*, a long *ee* as in 'week', or *yee* after a consonant
í	<u>*ee*</u>, a longer *ee* sound
o	*o*, a short *o* as in 'hot'
ó	<u>*o*</u>, like *au* in 'caught'
u	*oo* as in 'boot'
ú/ů	<u>*oo*</u>, a longer *oo* sound. These are the same letter but **ú** is generally used at the beginning of a word.
y/ý	pronounced the same as **i/í**

Czech consonants are generally pronounced as in English, but look out for the following transcriptions:

č	*ch* as in 'check'
ď	*dye*, like *di* in 'soldier'
h	a panting sound. At the end of a word, like *ch* in Scottish 'loch'
ch	as in Scottish 'loch'

6

j	*y* as in 'yes'. When it follows a vowel j can act like an English y, eg čaj (tea) *chay*. But in an initial position it is barely pronounced, eg jsem (I am) *sem*.
ň	*ny* as in 'canyon'
r	rolled, Scottish-style
ř	rolled, Scottish-style r combined with *zh* as in 'leisure'
š	*sh* as in 'ship'
ť	*ty*, like *ti* in 'prettier'
ž	*zh* as in 'leisure'

The letters **q**, **w** and **x** are only found in words of foreign origin.

Note that when a group of consonants occurs with no vowels in between, the letters **r** and **l** act like vowels, eg krk (neck) is pronounced rather like the Scottish 'kirk', with a rolled r.

Getting started

bye	ahoj *a-hoy*
excuse me	promiňte **pro**-mee-ny-te
goodbye	na shledanou *na* s-hle-da-no-oo
good evening	dobrý večer *do*-<u>bree</u> **ve**-cher
good morning	dobré ráno *do*-<u>bre</u> *ra*-no
goodnight	dobrou noc *do*-bro-oo nots
hello	dobrý den *do*-<u>bree</u> den
hi	ahoj *a*-hoy, čau *cha*-oo
no	ne *ne*
OK	ok *o*-key
pardon	pardon *par*-don
please	prosím vás **pro**-seem v<u>as</u>
thank you	děkuji *dye*-koo-yee
yes	ano *a*-no, jo yo

I'd like ...
rád (m)/ráda (f) bych ...
*r<u>a</u>d/**ra**-da beekh ...*

we'd like ...
rádi bychom ...
*r<u>a</u>d-yee **bee**-khom ...*

is there a ...?
je tady někde ...?
*ye **ta**-dee **nyek**-de ...?*

are there any ...?
jsou tady někde ...?
*ys<u>o</u>-oo **ta**-dee **nyek**-de ...?*

where is ...?
kde je ...?
kde ye ...?

where are ...?
kde jsou ...?
kde ys<u>o</u>-oo ...?

how much is it?
kolik to stojí?
***ko**-leek to **stoy**-<u>ee</u>?*

do you speak English?
mluvíte anglicky?
***mloo**-v<u>ee</u>-te **an**-gleet-skee?*

how are you?
jak se máš?
yak se m<u>a</u>sh?

fine, thanks
děkuju, dobře
***dyek**-oo-yoo, **dob**-rzhe*

what's your name?
jak se jmenuješ?
*yak se **ymen**-oo-yesh?*

my name's ...
jmenuji se ...
***ymen**-ooyee se ...*

where are you from?
odkud jsi?
*od-**kood** ysee?*

I'm from ...
jsem z ...
ysem z ...

yes, please
ano (prosím)
***a**-no (**pro**-s<u>ee</u>m)*

no, thanks
ne, děkuji
*ne, **dyek**-oo-yee*

thanks very much
mockrát děkuju
***mot**-skr<u>a</u>t **dyek**-oo-yoo*

you're welcome
není zač
***nen**-<u>ee</u> zach*

see you later
zatím nashledanou
za-teem nas-hle-da-no-oo

I'm sorry
je mi (to) líto
ye mee (to) lee-to

pardon?
prosím?
pro-seem?

what?
co?
tso?

I don't understand
nerozumím
ne-ro-zoo-meem

how do you say ... in Czech?
jak se řekne česky ...?
yak se rzhek-ne ches-kee ...?

could you repeat that, please?
můžete to říct ještě jednou?
moo-zhe-te to rzheetst yesh-tye yed-no-oo?

could you write it down for me?
mohl (m)/mohla (f) byste mi to napsat?
mohl/moh-la bee-ste mee to nap-sat?

I love you
miluju tě
meel-oo-yoo tye

shit!
do prdele!
do prd-e-le !

Reading signs

mimo provoz	out of order
obsazeno	occupied
otevřeno	open
pozor	attention
réservé	reserved
toalety	toilets
toalety muži	gents *(toilet)*
toalety ženy	ladies' *(toilet)*
vchod	entrance

východ	exit
zákaz kouření	no smoking
zákaz parkování	no parking
zavřeno	closed

Following directions

pořád rovně **porzh-**_ad_ **rov**-nye straight ahead
vlevo **vlev**-o left
vpravo **vprav**-o right

turn left/right
zahněte doleva/doprava
zah-nyete **do**-leva/**do**-prava

keep going straight on
jděte pořád rovně
y**dyet**-e **porzh**-_ad_ **rov**-nye

Language tips

- Czech has two ways of saying *you*: **ty** and **vy**. Use ty when speaking to a friend or young person, and vy when speaking to older people, in formal situations and when addressing more than one person (formally or informally). Note that the verb form will change accordingly. In this book we have used the ty form unless the context would make it inappropriate.
- Subject pronouns (*I, you, he* etc) are often omitted in Czech unless needed for emphasis, as the verb ending shows shows which person is meant.
- Czech has no definite or indefinite articles (*the, a/an*). However, all nouns belong to one of three genders, masculine, feminine or neuter.
- Adjectives generally come before the noun they describe and must agree with it in number, gender and case.
- Czech has seven cases: nouns take different cases depending on their function in the sentence, and their endings change accordingly.

- Note that **ano** (*yes*) is often abbreviated to **no** or **jo**, so **no** may actually mean yes! (Remember that **ne** means *no*.)

Numbers

0 nula *noo-la*
1 jedna *yed-na*
2 dva *dva*
3 tři *trzhee*
4 čtyři *chteer-zhee*
5 pět *pyet*
6 šest *shest*
7 sedm *sedm/sed-oom*
8 osm *osm/os-oom*
9 devět *dev-yet*
10 deset *de-set*
11 jedenáct *yed-en-atst*
12 dvanáct *dva-natst*
13 třináct *trzhee-natst*
14 čtrnáct *chtr-natst*
15 patnáct *pat-natst*
16 šestnáct *shest-natst*

17 sedmnáct *sedm-natst*
18 osmnáct *osm-natst*
19 devatenáct *dev-a-te-natst*
20 dvacet *dvat-set*
21 dvacet jedna *dvat-set yed-na*
30 třicet *trzheet-set*
40 čtyřicet *chteer-zheet-set*
50 padesát *pa-de-sat*
60 šedesát *she-de-sat*
70 sedmdesát *sedm-de-sat*
80 osmdesát *osm-de-sat*
90 devadesát *dev-a-de-sat*
100 sto *sto*
101 sto jedna *sto yed-na*
500 pět set *pyet set*
1000 tisíc *tee-seets*
1000 000 milión *mee-lee-on*

Danish

Alphabet and pronunciation

The Danish alphabet has 29 letters which are pronounced as follows. Note that the additional letters **æ**, **ø** and **å** are placed at the end of the alphabet, so if you have a Danish dictionary they will be found after z.

a *ah*	**k** *koe*	**u** *oo*
b *bay*	**l** *el*	**v** *vay*
c *say*	**m** *em*	**w** ***dobbel**-vay*
d *day*	**n** *en*	**x** *eks*
e *ay*	**o** *oh*	**y** *ui*
f *ef*	**p** *pay*	**z** *zet*
g *gay*	**q** *coo*	**æ** *e*
h *hoe*	**r** *er*	**ø** *eu*
i *ee*	**s** *es*	**å** *aw*
j *yoith*	**t** *tay*	

Consonants are generally pronounced as in English, but note the following points:

g   hard, as in 'guest' (not as in 'ginger'), unless the word is a loan word from English (eg 'gin')

j   always soft, like the *y* in 'yes' (not as in 'jam')

d   either hard (as in 'dog') or soft (the English equivalent would be *th* in 'the')

nd   a particular Danish consonant combination, used often – pronounced 'n'

ng   *as* in 'sing'

Vowels are slightly trickier:

o   a short, open sound, like the *u* in 'up'

| *y* | a long sound, like *ou* in 'you' |
| *u* | a long sound, like *oo* in 'boot' |

The three vowels special to Danish are pronounced as follows (they are all long sounds):

æ	*e* as in 'get'
ø	*eu*, similar to the last syllable of 'chauffeur'
å	the sound is somewhere between the *aw* of 'paw' and the *oe* of 'goes'. In this book, the transcription *aw* will be used.

Note also the following transcriptions used in this book:

TH	for Danish soft *d*, like *th* in 'the', but unvoiced – there is no expulsion of air
ai	like *i* in 'line'
ah	between short *a* and the *a* in 'bath' (as someone from southern England would pronounce it) – a short sound
eh	like *e* in 'get'
uh	like *e* in 'the'
oe	like *oe* in 'goes'
oh	between *u* in 'up' and the English *oh* sound – an open sound
ue	like *ou* in 'you'
aa	long *a* sound, as someone from southern England would pronounce 'bath'

Bare Essentials: Danish

Getting started

bye	hej hej *hai-hai*
excuse me	undskyld **uhn**-*skuel*
goodbye	farvel *fah-***vel**
good evening	godaften *go-***aaf***-tuhn*
good morning	godmorgen *go-***morn**
goodnight	godnat *go-***nat**
hello, hi	hej *hai*

no   nej *nai*
OK   okay *okay*
thanks, thank you   tak *tahk*
yes   ja *yah*

I'd like ...
jeg vil gerne have ...
*yai vil gern **ha**-uh ...*

we'd like ...
vi vil gerne have ...
*vee vil gern **ha**-uh ...*

is there/are there...?
er der ...?
ehr dehr ...?

where is/are ...?
hvor er ...?
vor ehr ...?

how much is it?
hvor meget koster det?
*vor **mai**-yuht **koss**-tuhr deh?*

do you speak English?
taler du engelsk?
*tal-uhr doo **eng**-uhlsk?*

what's your name?
hvad hedder du?
*vaTH **heTH**-uhr doo?*

my name's ...
jeg hedder ...
*yai **heTH**-uhr ...*

where are you from?
hvor kommer du fra?
*vor **kom**-muhr doo fraa?*

I'm from ...
jeg kommer fra ...
*yai **kom**-muhr fraa ...*

how are you?
hvordan går det?
*vor-**dann** gaw deh?*

fine, thanks
fint, tak
feent, tahk

yes, please
ja, tak
yah, tahk

no, thanks
nej, tak
nai, tahk

thanks very much
mange tak
***mahng**-uh tahk*

you're welcome
det var så lidt
deh vaar saw litt

14

see you later
vi ses
vee sehs

pardon?
hvad siger du?
va see-uhr doo?

could you repeat that, please?
vil du godt gentage?
vil doo gott gen-ta-yuh?

I don't understand
jeg forstår ikke
yai for-staw ik-kuh

I love you
jeg elsker dig
yai el-skuhr dai

I'm sorry
jeg er ked af det
yai er keTH a deh

what?
hvad?
vaTH?

how do you say ... in Danish?
hvad hedder ... på dansk?
va heTH-uhr ... paw dansk?

could you write it down for me?
kan du skrive det?
can doo skri-vuh deh?

shit!
pis!
pis!

Reading signs

advarsel	attention
dametoilet	ladies' *(toilet)*
herretoilet	gents *(toilet)*
indgang	entrance
lukket	closed
parkering forbudt	no parking
reserveret	reserved
rygning forbudt	no smoking
toilet	toilets
udgang	exit
åben	open

Bare Essentials: Danish

Following directions

højre *hoi-ruh* right
lige ud *leei-uh ooTH* straight on
venstre *ven-struh* left

turn left/right
drej til venstre/højre
*drai til **ven**-struh/**hoi**-ruh*

keep going straight on
forsæt lige ud
for-set lee-uh ooTH

Language tips

- There are two different words for *you* in Danish: **du**, used to address one person, and **I**, used to address more than one. In this book we have used du unless the context would make it inappropriate. The word **De** is a very formal term of address and is rarely used, so we have not used it in this book.
- All Danish nouns belong to one of two genders, common or neuter. The indefinite article (*a/an*) is **en** before singular common nouns and **et** before singular neuter (there is no indefinite article before plurals). The definite article (*the*) is tacked onto the end of the noun (**-en/-n** for common nouns, **-et/-t** for neuter): mand (*man*) > mand**en**, pige (*girl*) > pig**en**; hus (*house*) > hus**et**, æble (*apple*) > æbl**et**.
- To form indefinite plurals (eg *(some) cars*), simply add a plural ending to the noun. This is usually **-er** or **-e**, though there are exceptions: en student (*a student*) > student**er** (*students*), en dreng (*a boy*), dreng**e** (*boys*). To form definite plurals (eg *the cars*), add the plural ending followed by **-ne**: student**er** (*students*) > student**erne** (*the students*), dreng**e** (*boys*) > dreng**ene** (*the boys*).
- Danish has no word for *please*: when asking for something politely, you can use an expression like Jeg vil gerne bede om ... (literally *I would like to ask for ...*), and end your sentence with an added tak (*thank you*).

Numbers

0 nul *nuhll*
1 en *ehn*
2 to *toh*
3 tre *trey*
4 fire *fee-ruh*
5 fem *fem*
6 seks *sex*
7 syv *suev*
8 otte *oett-uh*
9 ni *nee*
10 ti *tee*
11 elleve *ell-uh-vuh*
12 tolv *toll*
13 tretten *tra-tuhn*
14 fjorten *fjohr-tuhn*
15 femten *fem-tuhn*
16 seksten *sais-tuhn*
17 sytten *sue-tuhn*
18 atten *a-tuhn*

19 nitten *ni-tuhn*
20 tyve *tue-vuh*
21 enogtyve *eyn-o-tue-vuh*
22 toogtyve *toh-o-tue-vuh*
30 tredive *traiTH-vuh*
40 fyrre *fue-ruh*
50 halvtreds *hal-tress*
60 tres *tress*
70 halvfjerds *hal-fjerss*
80 firs *feers*
90 halvfems *hal-fems*
100 hundrede *hun-ruh-THuh*
101 hundrede og en *hun-ruh-THuh-o-eyn*
500 fem hundrede *fem hun-ruh-THuh*
1000 tusind *too-sinn*
1000000 million *mil-i-yohn*

Dutch

Alphabet and pronunciation

The letters of the Dutch alphabet are pronounced as follows:

a *ah*	**j** *yay*	**s** *ess*
b *bay*	**k** *kah*	**t** *tay*
c *say*	**l** *el*	**u** *oo*
d *day*	**m** *em*	**v** *vay*
e *ay*	**n** *en*	**w** *way*
f *ef*	**o** *oh*	**x** *eeks*
g *CHay*	**p** *pay*	**y** *eh-ee*
h *hah*	**q** *koo*	**z** *zet*
i *ee*	**r** *air*	

We have used the following transcriptions to help you pronounce unfamiliar Dutch sounds:

CH   like the *ch* in Scottish 'loch'
zh   as in 'leisure'
uu   try making the sound *ee* and then pursing your lips

Dutch vowels may be short or long; note the different pronunciations and the transcriptions used in this book:

a   *a* similar to *u* in 'cut' / *ah* as in 'bar'
e   *eh* as in 'pet' / *ay* as in 'pay'
       e as in 'the'
i   *i* as in 'sip' / *ee* as in 'tree'
o   *o* as in 'hot' / *oh* as in 'phone'
u   *e* as in 'the' / *uu* see above

Note the following combinations of vowels:
aai   *eye* as in 'eye': lawaai *la-***veye** (noise)

au, ou	*ow* as in 'towel': mevrouw me-**vrow** (Madam)
ei, ij	*ay* as in 'pay': plein *playn* (place), vijf *vayf* (five)
ie	*ee* as in 'feel': drie *dree* (three)
oe	*oo* as in 'food': boek *book* (book)
ooi	*oo-ee* like the *oui* in 'Louise': mooi **moo**-ee (pretty)
ui	*eui*, no equivalent in English – try saying *ow* as in 'town' with the lips and the tongue pressed down: huis *heuis* (house)

Most consonants are pronounced as in English, but note the following pronunciation tips:

b, d	pronounced *p* and *t* respectively at the end of a word: ik heb *ik hehp* (I have); bed *bet* (bed)
ch, g	pronounced *CH* (see above): goed *CHoht* (good)
j	pronounced *y* as in 'yes': jij *yay* (you)
n	when words end in -en, the final n is not usually pronounced and we have shown it in brackets: spreken **spray**-*ke(n)* (to speak)
r	pronounced in the back of the throat, as in French
sj	pronounced *sh*: meisje **maysh**-*e* (girl)
v	at the start of a word, or after b, ch, d, f, g, p or s, pronounced *f* as in 'fun'
	in other positions, pronounced v as in 'vodka'
w	at the end of a word, pronounced *w* as in 'water'
	in other positions, pronounced v as in 'vodka'
z	after b, ch, d, f, g, k, p, s or t, pronounced *s* as in 'sip'
	in other positions, pronounced *z* as in 'zoo'

Getting started

bye	dag *dahCH*
excuse me	pardon *par-***dohn**
good afternoon	goedemiddag *CHoo-de-***mid**-*aCH*
goodbye	tot ziens *tot* **seens**
good evening	goedenavond *CHoo-den-***ah**-*vont*

19

good morning	goedemorgen *CHoo-de-**mor**-CHe(n)*
goodnight	goedenacht *CHoo-de-**naCHt***
hello	hallo *ha-**loh***
hi	dag *dahCH*
no	nee *nay*
OK	ok *oh-**kay***
please	alstublieft *als-too-**bleeft***
thanks	bedankt *be-**dankt***
thank you	dank u wel *dank oo **well***
yes	ja *yah*

Bare Essentials: Dutch

I'd like ...
ik zou graag ...
ik zow CHrahCH ...

we'd like ...
wij zouden graag ...
*vay **zow**-de(n) CHrahCH ...*

is there ...?
is er een ...?
is ehr en ...?

are there ...?
zijn er...?
zayn ehr ...?

where is ...?
waar is ...?
vahr is ...?

where are ...?
waar zijn ...?
vahr zayn ...?

how much is it?
hoeveel kost het?
*hoo-**vayl** kost het?*

do you speak English?
spreekt je Engels?
*spraykt ye **ehng**-els?*

what's your name?
hoe heet jij?
hoo hayt yay?

my name's ...
ik heet ...
ik hayt ...

where are you from?
waar kom je vandaan?
*vahr kom ye van-**dahn**?*

I'm from ...
ik kom uit ...
ik kom euit ...

how are you?
hoe gaat het met je?
hoo CHaht het meht ye?

fine, thanks
goed, dank je
CHoot, dank ye

yes, please
ja, graag
yah, CHrahCH

no, thanks
nee, bedankt
nay, be-dankt

thanks very much
hartelijk dank
hart-e-lek dank

you're welcome
graag gedaan
CHrahCH CHe-dahn

see you later
tot later
tot laht-er

I'm sorry
het spijt me/sorry
het spayt me/sor-ree

pardon?
sorry?
sor-ree?

what?
wat?
vat?

could you repeat that, please?
kunt je dat herhalen, alstublieft?
kent ye dat hehr-hahl-e(n), als-too-bleeft?

how do you say ... in Dutch?
hoe zeg je ... in het Nederlands?
hoo zehCH ye ... in het nayd-er-lands?

I don't understand
ik begrijp het niet
ik be-CHrayp het neet

could you write it down for me?
kunt je dat voor mij opschrijven?
kent ye dat for may op-sCHrayv-e(n)

I love you
ik hou van jou
ik how van yow

shit!
shit!
shit!

Reading signs

dames	ladies' *(toilet)*
geopend	open
gereserveerd	reserved
gesloten	closed
heren	gents *(toilet)*
ingang	entrance
open	open
pas op	attention
toiletten	toilets
uitgang	exit
verboden te parkeren	no parking
verboden te roken	no smoking

Following directions

links *links* left
rechtdoor *rehCHt-dor* straight ahead
rechts *rehCHts* right

turn left/right
linksaf/rechtsaf
links-af/rehCHts-af

keep going straight on
rechtdoor
rehCHt-dohr

Language tips

• Dutch has different ways of saying *you*: **je**, **u** and **jullie**. Je is generally used when speaking to a young person or friend, and u when speaking to an older person or in formal situations; however the rules are fairly relaxed. Jullie is used to address more than one person, formally or informally. Note that the verb form will change accordingly. In this book we have used the je form unless the context would make it inappropriate.

- All Dutch nouns belong to one of three genders, masculine, feminine and neuter. The definite article (*the*) is **de** before masculine and feminine singular nouns and **het** before neuter; **de** is also used before plurals. The indefinite article (*a/an*) is **een** before all singular nouns (there is no indefinite article before plurals).
- Most plurals are formed by adding **-en**.

Numbers

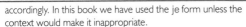

0 nul *nel*
1 één *ayn*
2 twee *tway*
3 drie *dree*
4 vier *feer*
5 vijf *fayf*
6 zes *zehs*
7 zeven *zay-ve(n)*
8 acht *aCHt*
9 negen *nay-CHe(n)*
10 tien *teen*
11 elf *ehlf*
12 twaalf *twahlf*
13 dertien *dehr-teen*
14 veertien *vayr-teen*
15 vijftien *vayf-teen*
16 zestien *zehs-teen*
17 zeventien *zay-ven-teen*
18 achttien *aCHt-teen*

19 negentien *nay-CHen-teen*
20 twintig *twin-teCH*
21 eenentwintig *ayn-en-twin-teCH*
22 tweeëntwintig *tway-en-twin-teCH*
30 dertig *dehr-teCH*
40 veertig *vayr-teCH*
50 vijftig *vayf-teCH*
60 zestig *zehs-teCH*
70 zeventig *zay-ven-teCH*
80 tachtig *taCH-teCH*
90 negentig *nay-CHen-tech*
100 honderd *hond-ert*
101 honderdeneen *hond-erd-en-ayn*
500 vijfhonderd *fayf-hond-ert*
1000 duizend *deuiz-ent*
1000000 één miljoen *ayn mil-yoon*

French

Unlike English, French puts roughly equal stress on all the syllables of a word, so we have not used bold to show stress as for other languages.

Alphabet and pronunciation

The French alphabet is essentially the same as the English one. The letters are pronounced as follows:

a *ah*	**j** *zhee*	**s** *ess*
b *bay*	**k** *kah*	**t** *tay*
c *say*	**l** *ell*	**u** *U*
d *day*	**m** *emm*	**v** *vay*
e *ay*	**n** *enn*	**w** *doo-bluh-vay*
f *ef*	**o** *oh*	**x** *eeks*
g *zhay*	**p** *pay*	**y** *ee-grek*
h *ash*	**q** *kU*	**z** *zed*
i *ee*	**r** *air*	

French also has some accented vowels which are pronounced as follows:

à, â	*a* (as in 'cat')
é	*ay* (as in 'pay')
è, ê	*e* (as in 'pet')

We have used the following codes to transcribe unfamiliar French sounds. The first two are nasal sounds, ie they are produced more through the nose than the mouth.

ON   For the nasalised sounds **on**, **en**, **em**, **an** and **am** and a few other combinations in French. Try saying the English word 'gong' and stopping short of pronouncing the full *ng* sound, eg bon *bON* (good), entrée *ON-tray* (entrance), santé *sON-tay* (health), ambassade *ON-ba-sad* (embassy)

AN	For the nasalised sounds **un** and **in**, and a few other combinations in French. Try saying the English word 'van' and stopping just short of pronouncing the 'n', eg: quelqu'un *kel-kAN* (someone), vin *vAN* (wine)
U	To pronounce the written French **u**, try pursing your lips and then trying to make an ee sound. Try not to confuse this with the written French **ou**, which is pronounced simply *oo* as in 'cool': bus *bUs*, as opposed to route *root* (road)
ey	Used to show the pronunciation of -**eil** and -**eille**, rather as in the English 'survey' but slightly pronouncing the ee sound of the y at the end, eg bouteille *boo-tey* (bottle)
oy	Used to show the pronunciation of the combination -**euil**, rather as in the English 'boy' but slightly pronouncing the ee sound of the y at the end, eg fauteuil *fau-toy* (armchair)
uh	Used to show the pronunciation of **e**, **eu** and some other combinations in certain words: le *luh* (the), feu *fuh* (fire), œuf *uhf* (egg)
zh	Used to show the pronunciation of **j** and soft **g**. This sound is just like the s in the English word 'pleasure', eg jaloux *zha-loo* (jealous), plage *plazh* (beach)

Some consonants are pronounced differently in French:

h	not generally pronounced: habiter *a-bee-tay* (to live)
qu	like *k* in 'king': quai *kay* (platform)
r	vibrated at the back of your throat
w	like *v* in 'vote': wagon *va-gON* (coach – on train)

A few common French word endings and how to pronounce them:

-at	*-ah*	**-ez**	*-ay*
-eau	*-oh*	**-ot**	*-oh*
-et	*-ay*		

Note that the **-s** plural ending is not usually pronounced in French: chats *sha* (cats).

When a French word ends in **-re** or **-le**, you normally stop just short of pronouncing the final e as a separate syllable. We have shown this as follows: être *etr* (to be), prendre *prONdr* (to take), spectacle *spek-takl* (show).

Getting started

bye	salut *sa-lU*
excuse me	excusez-moi *ek-sku-zay-mwa*
good afternoon	bonjour *bON-zhoor*
goodbye	au revoir *oh ruh-vwar*
good evening	bonsoir *bON-swar*
good morning	bonjour *bON-zhoor*
goodnight	bonne nuit *bon nwee*
hello	bonjour *bON-zhoor*
hi	salut *sa-lU*
no	non *nON*
OK	d'accord *da-kor*, ok *oh-kay*
please	*(formal)* s'il vous plaît *seel voo play*, *(informal)* s'il te plaît *seel tuh play*
thanks, thank you	merci *mair-see*
yes	oui *wee*

I'd like ...
je voudrais ...
zhuh voo-dray ...

we'd like ...
nous voudrions ...
noo voo-dree-yON ...

where is ...?
où est ... ?
oo ay ...?

where are ...?
où sont ... ?
oo sON ...?

is there/are there ...?
est-ce qu'il y a ... ?
ess keel ya ...?

how much is it?
c'est combien ?
say kON-byAN?

do you speak English?
est-ce que vous parlez anglais ?
ess kuh voo par-lay ON-glay?

how are you?
comment ça va ?
ko-mON sa va?

fine, thanks
bien, merci
byAN, mair-see

what's your name?
comment t'appelles-tu ?
ko-mON ta-pell-tU ?

my name's ...
je m'appelle ...
zhuh ma-pell ...

where are you from?
d'où viens tu?
doo vyAN tU?

I'm from ...
je viens de ...
zhuh vyAN duh ...

yes, please
oui, merci
wee, mair-see

no, thanks
non merci
nON mair-see

thanks very much
merci beaucoup
mair-see boh-koo

you're welcome
de rien
de ree-AN

see you later
à tout à l'heure
a toot a luhr

I'm sorry
je suis désolé
zhuh swee day-zoh-lay

pardon?
pardon ?
par-dON?

what?
quoi ?
kwa?

I don't understand
je ne comprends pas
zhuh nuh kON-prON pa

could you repeat that, please?
vous pouvez répéter, s'il vous plaît ?
voo poo-vay ray-pay-tay, seel voo play?

Bare Essentials: French

how do you say … in French?
comment dit-on … en français ?
ko-mON deet ON … ON frON-say?

could you write it down for me?
est-ce que vous pourriez me l'écrire ?
ess kuh voo poo-ree-ay muh lay-kreer?

I love you
je t'aime
zhuh tem

shit!
merde !
maird!

Reading signs

attention	warning
dames	ladies *(toilet)*
défense de fumer	no smoking
entrée	entrance
hommes	gents *(toilet)*
hors service	out of order
ouvert	open
réservé	reserved
sortie	exit
stationnement interdit	no parking
toilettes	toilets

Following directions

gauche *gohsh* left
droite *drwat* right
tout droit *too drwa* straight ahead

turn left/right
tournez à gauche/à droite
toor-nay a gohsh/a drwat

keep going straight ahead
continuez tout droit
kON-tee-nU-ay too drwa

Language tips

- French has two ways of saying *you*: **tu** and **vous**. Use tu when speaking to a friend or young person and vous when addressing older people or people you don't know, and in formal contexts. Vous is also used when addressing more than one person (formally or informally). Note that the verb form will change accordingly. In this book we have used the tu form unless the context would make it inappropriate.
- All French nouns are either masculine (*m*) or feminine (*f*) in gender. The definite article (*the*) is **le** before masculine singular nouns, **la** before feminine singular or **l'** before any singular noun beginning with a vowel. **Les** is used before plural nouns. The indefinite article (*a/an*) is **un** before masculine singular nouns, **une** for feminine singular and **des** (*some*) for plural.
- Adjectives agree with the gender and number of the noun they describe and their endings may change accordingly.

Bare Essentials: French

Numbers

0 zéro *zay-roh*

1 un *AN*

2 deux *duh*

3 trois *trwa*

4 quatre *katr*

5 cinq *sANk*

6 six *sees*

7 sept *set*

8 huit *weet*

9 neuf *nuhf*

10 dix *dees*

11 onze *ONz*

12 douze *dooz*

13 treize *trez*

14 quatorze *ka-torz*

15 quinze *kANz*

29

16 seize *sez*
17 dix-sept *dees-set*
18 dix-huit *deez-weet*
19 dix-neuf *deez-nuhf*
20 vingt *vAN*
21 vingt et un *vAN-tay-AN*
22 vingt-deux *vAN-duh*
30 trente *trONt*
40 quarante *ka-rONt*
50 cinquante *sAN-kONt*
60 soixante *swa-sONt*

70 soixante-dix *swa-sONt-dees*
80 quatre-vingts *ka-truh-vAN*
90 quatre-vingt-dix *ka-truh-vAN-dees*
100 cent *sON*
101 cent un *sON-AN*
500 cinq cents *sANk sON*
1000 mille *meel*
1000 000 un million *AN meel-yON*

German

Alphabet and pronunciation

The letters of the German alphabet are pronounced as follows:

a *ah*	**j** *yot*	**s** *ess*
b *bay*	**k** *kah*	**t** *tay*
c *tsay*	**l** *el*	**u** *oo*
d *day*	**m** *em*	**v** *fow*
e *ay*	**n** *en*	**w** *vay*
f *ef*	**o** *oh*	**x** *iks*
g *gay*	**p** *pay*	**y** ***uup**-si-lon*
h *hah*	**q** *koo*	**z** *tset*
i *ee*	**r** *err*	

The following transcriptions have been used to help you pronounce German vowels correctly:

a as in 'cat'	*e* as in 'pet'	*i* as in 'sip'	*o* as in 'hot'
ah as in 'bar'	*ee* as in 'tree'	*u* as in 'push'	*oo* as in 'pool'
ay as in 'pay'	*ehr* as in 'hair'	*uh* as in 'the'	*ow* as in 'town'
ey as in 'eye'	*oy* as in 'boy'		

German also has the letters **ä**, **ö** and **ü**, which are pronounced differently from the regular vowels; they have been transcribed as follows:

ä e as in 'get' / *eh*, the same sound but longer:
Männer **men**-*uh* (men) / fährt *fehrt* (drives, goes)

ö *eu*: similar to the last syllable of 'chauffeur'. May be short (*eu*) or long (<u>*eu*</u>):
können **keun**-*uhn* (to be able to) / schön *sh<u>eu</u>n* (beautiful)

ü *uu*: try making the sound ee and then pursing your lips. May be short (*uu*) or long (<u>*uu*</u>):
fünf *fuunf* (five) / süß *z<u>uus</u>* (sweet)

31

Consonants are generally pronounced as in English, but note the following points:

g	always hard, as in 'guest' (not as in 'ginger')
r	pronounced in the back of the throat, similar to the Scottish 'loch' sound
v	pronounced f as in 'fun'
w	pronounced v as in 'vodka'

Some German sounds do not exist in English and we have used the following codes to transcribe them:

CH	as in Scottish 'loch'
oh	try making the sound o and then pursing your lips – similar to a Northern English or Scottish person saying 'phone'

Getting started

bye	tschüß *tshuus*
excuse me	Entschuldigung *ent-**shul**-di-gung*
good afternoon	guten Tag *goo-tuhn tahk*
goodbye	auf Wiedersehen *owf **vee**-duh-zayn*
good evening	guten Abend *goo-tuhn **ah**-buhnt*
good morning	guten Morgen *goo-tuhn **mor**-guhn*
goodnight	gute Nacht *goo-tuh naCHt*
hello, hi	hallo *ha-loh*
no	nein *neyn*
OK	okay *oh-**kay***
please	bitte *bit-uh*
thanks, thank you	danke *dang-kuh*
yes	ja *yah*

I'd like ...	**we'd like ...**
ich möchte ...	wir möchten ...
*ish **meush**-tuh ...*	*veer **meush**-tuhn ...*

is there/are there ...?
gibt es ...?
geept ess ...?

how much is it?
wie viel kostet das?
vee feel kos-tuht das?

where is ...?
wo ist ...?
voh ist ...?

where are ...?
wo sind ...?
voh zint ...?

do you speak English?
sprechen Sie Englisch?
shpre-shuhn zee eng-lish?

what's your name?
wie heißt du?
vee heyst doo?

my name's ...
ich heiße ...
ish hey-suh ...

where are you from?
woher kommst du?
voh-hehr komst doo?

I'm from ...
ich komme aus ...
ish kom-uh ows ...

how are you?
wie geht's?
vee gayts?

fine, thanks
danke, gut
dang-kuh, goot

yes, please
ja, bitte
yah, bit-uh

no, thanks
nein, danke
neyn, dang-kuh

thanks very much
vielen Dank
fee-luhn dank

you're welcome
bitte
bit-uh

see you later
bis später
bis shpeh-tuh

I'm sorry
es tut mir Leid
ess toot meer leyt

pardon?	**what?**
wie bitte?	was?
*vee **bit**-uh?*	*vas?*

I don't understand	**how do you say ... in German?**
ich verstehe nicht	was heißt ... auf Deutsch?
*ish fehr-**shtay**-uh nisht*	*vas heyst ... owf doytsh?*

could you repeat that, please?
könnten Sie das bitte wiederholen?
*keun-tuhn zee das **bit**-uh vee-duh-**hoh**-luhn?*

could you write it down for me?
könnten Sie mir das bitte aufschreiben?
*keun-tuhn zee meer das **bit**-uh **owf**-shrhey-buhn?*

I love you	**shit!**
ich liebe Dich	Scheiße!
*ish **lee**-buh dish*	***shey**-suh!*

Reading signs

Achtung	attention, be careful
Ausgang	exit
außer Betrieb	out of order
Damen	ladies' *(toilet)*
Eingang	entrance
geöffnet	open
geschlossen	closed
Herren	gents' *(toilet)*
Parken verboten	no parking
Rauchen verboten	no smoking
reserviert	reserved
Toiletten	toilets

Following directions

geradeaus *guh-rah-duh-**ows*** straight ahead
links *links* left
rechts *reshts* right

turn left/right
biegen Sie links/rechts ab
bee-guhn zee links/reshts ab

go straight ahead
gehen Sie geradeaus
*gay-uhn zee guh-rah-duh-**ows***

Language tips

- German has different ways of saying *you*: **du**, **ihr** and **Sie**. Use du when speaking to a friend or young person, and Sie with older people or in formal situations. When addressing more than one person, use ihr in informal situations and Sie in formal ones. Note that the verb form will change accordingly. In this book we have used the du form unless the context would make it inappropriate.
- All German nouns belong to one of three genders, masculine, feminine and neuter. The definite article (*the*) is **der** before singular masculine nouns, **die** before feminine ones and **das** before neuter ones. In the plural, **die** is used for all genders. The indefinite article (*a/an*) is **ein** before masculine or neuter nouns, and **eine** before feminine ones. However, you will see nouns and articles written with different endings – this is because they are in a different case. German has four cases: nominative (for the subject of the sentence), accusative (for the direct object), dative (for the indirect object) and genitive (for possession).
- In written German, the letter **ß** is often used to replace a double s after a long vowel. And don't be surprised at the number of capital letters: all German nouns take an initial capital.

Numbers

0 null *nul*
1 eins *eyns*
2 zwei *tsvey*
3 drei *drey*
4 vier *feer*
5 fünf *fuunf*
6 sechs *zeks*
7 sieben *zee-buhn*
8 acht *aCHt*
9 neun *noyn*
10 zehn *tsayn*
11 elf *elf*
12 zwölf *tsveulf*
13 dreizehn *drey-tsayn*
14 vierzehn *feer-tsayn*
15 fünfzehn *fuunf-tsayn*
16 sechzehn *zeCH-tsayn*
17 siebzehn *zeep-tsayn*
18 achtzehn *aCH-tsayn*

19 neunzehn *noyn-tsayn*
20 zwanzig *tsvan-tsish*
21 einundzwanzig *eyn-unt-tsvan-tsish*
22 zweiundzwanzig *tsvey-unt-tsvan-tsish*
30 dreißig *drey-sish*
40 vierzig *feer-tsish*
50 fünfzig *fuunf-tsish*
60 sechzig *zeCH-tsish*
70 siebzig *zeep-tsish*
80 achtzig *aCH-tsish*
90 neunzig *noyn-tsish*
100 hundert *hun-dehrt*
101 hunderteins *hun-dehrt-eyns*
500 fünf hundert *fuunf hun-dehrt*
1000 tausend *tow-zuhnt*
1000 000 eine Million *ey-nuh mil-yohn*

Greek

Alphabet and pronunciation

Once you have mastered the alphabet, Greek is quite straightforward to read. The Greek alphabet has 24 letters which are pronounced as follows:

A α *al-pha*   *a* (as in 'bar')
B β *vi-ta*   *v*
Γ γ *gha-ma*   *gh*
  before ε or ι: *y* (as in 'yes')
  before γ and κ: *g* (as in 'game')
Δ δ *thel-ta*   *th* (as in 'this')
E ε *ep-si-lon*   *e* (as in egg)
Z ζ *zi-ta*   *z*
H η *i-ta*   *i* (as in 'sip')
Θ θ *THi-ta*   *TH* (as in 'thing')
I ι *yi-o-ta*   *i* (as in 'sip')
K κ *kapp-a*   *k*
Λ λ *lam-tha*   *l*
M μ *mi*   *m*
N ν *ni*   *n*
Ξ ξ *ksi*   *x*
O o *o-mi-cron*   *o* (as in 'hot')
Π π *pi*   *p*
P ρ *ro*   *r*
Σ σ *sigh-ma*   before μπ, ντ, ζ, μ, ν, ρ, β: *z*
(ς at end of word)   everywhere else: *s*
T τ *taf*   *t*
Y υ *ip-si-lon*   *i* (as in 'sip')
Φ φ *fi*   *f*
X χ *hi*   *h*

Ψ ψ *psi*   *ps* (as in 'lapse')
Ω ω *om-e-gha*   *o* as in 'hot'

Note particularly the following transcriptions used in this book:
gh   this sound is midway between the g in 'go' and the ch in Scottish 'loch'
TH   *th* as in 'thing' (as opposed to *th* in 'this', transcribed as *th*)

Note also the pronunciation of the following combinations of letters:

αι   *e* as in 'egg': παίζω *pe-zo* (I play)
ει   *i* as in 'sip': είμαι *i-me* (I am)
οι   *i* as in 'sip': οίκος *i-kos* (home)
υι   *i* as in 'sip': υιός *i-os* (son)
αυ   *av*: αύριο *av-rio* (tomorrow)
        af: αυτί *af-ti* (ear)
ευ   *ev*: Ευρώπη *Ev-ro-pi* (Europe)
        ef: ευτυχία *Ef-ti-hi-a* (happiness)
ου   *oo*: ουρανός *oo-ra-nos* (sky)
γκ   *g* as in 'game': γκάφα *ga-fa* (blunder)
γγ   *ng* as in 'finger': φεγγάρι *fen-ga-ri* (moon)
μπ   *b*: μπαμπάς *ba-bas* (daddy)
ντ   *d*: ντύνω *di-no* (to dress)
τσ   *ts*: τσάι *tsai* (tea)
τζ   *tz*: τζάκι *tza-ki* (fireplace)

Getting started

bye	γειά *ya*
excuse me	συγνώμη sigh-***no***-*mi*
good afternoon	καλό απόγευμα *ka-lo a-***po***-yev-ma*
goodbye	γειά *ya*, αντίο *a-***di***-o*
good evening	καλησπέρα *ka-li-***spe***-ra*
good morning	καλημέρα *ka-li-***me***-ra*

Bare Essentials: Greek

goodnight	καληνύχτα *ka-li-ni-hta*
hello, hi	γειά *ya*
no	όχι *o-hi*
OK	εντάξει *e-da-xi*, OK *OK*
pardon	συγνώμη *sigh-no-mi*
please	παρακαλώ *pa-ra-ka-lo*
thanks, thank you	ευχαριστώ *ef-ha-ri-sto*, σ'ευχαριστώ *sef-ha-ris-to*
yes	ναι *ne*

I'd like ...
θα ήθελα ...
THa i-THe-la ...

we'd like ...
θα θέλαμε ...
THa THe-la-me ...

is there a ...?
υπάρχει ένα ...;
i-pa-rhi e-na ...?

are there any ...?
υπάρχουν καθόλου ...;
i-par-hoon ka-THo-loo ...?

where is/are ...?
πού είναι ...;
poo i-ne ...?

how much is it?
πόσο κάνει;
po-so ka-ni?

how are you?
πώς είσαι;
pos i-se?

fine, thanks
καλά, ευχαριστώ
ka-la, ef-ha-ri-sto

what's your name?
ποιό είναι τ'όνομά σου;
pi-o i-ne to-no-ma soo?

my name's ...
τ'όνομά μου είναι ...
to-nom-a moo i-ne ...

where are you from?
από πού είστε;
a-po poo is-te?

I'm from ...
είμαι από ...
i-me a-po ...

Bare Essentials: Greek

yes, please
ναι, παρακαλώ
ne, pa-ra-ka-lo

no, thanks
όχι, ευχαριστώ
o-hi, ef-ha-ri-sto

thanks very much
ευχαριστώ πολύ
ef-ha-ri-sto po-li

you're welcome
παρακαλώ
pa-ra-ka-lo

see you later
θα σε δω αργότερα
THa se tho ar-gho-te-ra

I'm sorry
λυπάμαι
li-pa-me

pardon?
παρακαλώ;
pa-ra-ka-lo?

what?
τι;
ti?

could you repeat that, please?
μπορείτε να το επαναλάβετε αυτό, παρακαλώ;
bo-ri-te na to e-pa-na-la-ve-te af-to, pa-ra-ka-lo?

I don't understand
δεν καταλαβαίνω
then ka-ta-la-ve-no

do you speak English?
μιλάτε Αγγλικά;
mi-la-te ang-li-ka?

how do you say ... in Greek?
πώς λέτε ... στα ελληνικά;
pos le-te ... sta el-in-i-ka?

could you write it down for me?
μπορείτε να μου το γράψετε;
bo-ri-te na moo to ghra-pse-te?

I love you
σ'αγαπώ
sa-gha-po

shit!
σκατά!
ska-ta!

40

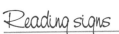

Reading signs

προσοχή	attention
κλειστό	closed
είσοδος	entrance
έξοδος	exit
ανδρών	gents *(toilet)*
γυναικών	ladies' *(toilet)*
δεν επιτρέπεται η στάθμευση	no parking
δεν επιτρέπεται το κάπνισμα	no smoking
ανοιχτά	open
εκτός λειτουργίας	out of order
ρεζερβέ	reserved
τουαλέτες	toilets

Following directions

αριστερά *a-ri-ste-ra* left
δεξιά *the-xi-a* right
ίσια *i-si-a* straight ahead

turn left/right
στρίψτε αριστερά/δεξιά
stri-pste a-ri-ste-ra/the-xi-a

keep going straight on
συνεχίστε όλο ευθεία
si-ne-hi-ste o-lo ef-THi-a

Language tips

- Greek has two ways of saying *you*: **εσύ** e-*si* and **εσείς** e-**sis**. The general rule is to use εσύ when speaking to a young person or someone you know well, and εσείς when speaking to older people or those in authority, though usage is relaxed and you may find even strangers address you informally. εσείς is also used to address more than one person (formally or informally). In this book we have used the informal option unless the context would make it inappropriate.

- Subject pronouns (*I, you, he* etc) are often omitted in Greek unless needed for emphasis, as the verb ending shows which person is meant.
- All Greek nouns belong to one of three genders: masculine, feminine and neuter. Greek also has four cases: nominative (for the subject of a sentence), accusative (for the object), genitive (used to show possession) and vocative (used to address someone). Noun endings and articles (*the, a/an*) change according to the gender and case used.
- Adjectives agree in number, gender and case with the noun they describe.
- Note that in written Greek a semi-colon is used instead of a question mark.

Numbers

0 μηδέν *mi-then*	**12** δώδεκα *tho-the-ka*
1 ένα *e-na*	**13** δεκατρία *the-ka-tri-a*
2 δύο *thi-o*	**14** δεκατέσσερα *the-ka-te-se-ra*
3 τρία *tri-a*	**15** δεκαπέντε *the-ka-pe-de*
4 τέσσερα *te-se-ra*	**16** δεκαέξι *the-ka-e-xi*
5 πέντε *pe-de*	**17** δεκαεπτά *the-ka-ep-ta*
6 έξι *ex-i*	**18** δεκαοχτώ *the-ka-oh-to*
7 επτά *ep-ta*	**19** δεκαεννιά *the-ka-e-ni-a*
8 οχτώ *oh-to*	**20** είκοσι *i-ko-si*
9 εννιά *e-ni-a*	**21** είκοσι ένα *i-ko-si e-na*
10 δέκα *the-ka*	**22** είκοσι δύο *i-ko-si thi-o*
11 έντεκα *e-de-ka*	**30** τριάντα *tri-a-da*

40 σαράντα *sa-ra-da*
50 πενήντα *pe-ni-da*
60 εξήντα *ex-i-da*
70 εβδομήντα *ev-tho-mi-da*
80 ογδόντα *og-tho-da*
90 εννενήντα *e-ne-ni-da*

100 εκατό *e-ka-to*
101 εκατόν ένα *e-ka-ton e-na*
500 πεντακόσια *pe-da-ko-sia*
1000 χίλια *hi-li-a*
1000 000 ένα εκατομύριο *e-na*
   e-ka-to-mi-ri-o

Italian

Alphabet and pronunciation

The Italian alphabet has 21 letters which are pronounced as follows:

a *ah*	**h** *ack-a*	**q** *koo*
b *bee*	**i** *ee*	**r** *err-ray*
c *chee*	**l** *el-lay*	**s** *ess-ay*
d *dee*	**m** *em-may*	**t** *tee*
e *ay*	**n** *en-nay*	**u** *oo*
f *ef-fay*	**o** *oh*	**v** *voo*
g *jee*	**p** *pee*	**z** *dzay-ta*

You sometimes find the letters **j** (ee *loong-ga*), **k** (*kap-a*), **w** (*dop-ee-ah voo*), **x** (*eeks*) and **y** (*eep-see-lon*) in words of foreign origin.

The following tips will help you to pronounce Italian words correctly.

When **c** and **g** come before **a**, **o** or **u**, they have a hard sound:
casa *kah-za* (house)   gasato *ga-zah-toh* (fizzy)
colore *kol-or-ay* (colour)   lago *lah-goh* (lake)
cucina *koo-chee-na* (kitchen)   gusto *goos-toh* (taste)

When they come before **e** or **i**, **c** is pronounced *ch* and **g** is pronounced *j*:
celebre *chel-ay-bray* (famous)   gente *jen-tay* (people)
cinema *chee-nay-ma* (cinema)   girasole *jee-ra-soh-lay* (sunflower)

When there is an **i** between the consonants **c** or **g** and the vowels **a**, **o**, or **u**, they are also pronounced *ch* and *j*:
ciao *chow* (hi/bye)   giardino *jar-dee-noh* (garden)
cioccolata *cho-koh-lah-ta*   giornale *jor-nah-lay* (newspaper)
(chocolate)

When there is an **h** between the consonants **c** or **g** and the vowels **e** and **i**, they are pronounced with a hard sound:

anche *ang-kay* (also)
spaghetti *spa-get-tee*
chiave *kee-ah-vay* (key)
ghiaccio *gee-a-choh* (ice)

R is always rolled.

Sca, **sco**, **scu**, **schi**, **sche** are pronounced *ska, sko, skoo, skee, skay*:

scarpe *skar-pay* (shoes)
sconto *skon-toh* (discount)
scusi *skoo-zee* (pardon)
schiaffo *skee-af-foh* (slap)
scherzo *sker-tzoh* (joke)

Sce and **sci** are pronounced *shay* and *shee*:

scena *shay-na* (scene)
sci *shee* (ski, skiiing)

Gli is pronounced *ly* as in the English word 'million':

moglie *mo-lyay* (wife)

Z is pronounced as *dz* in some words and as *ts* in others:

zona *dzoh-na* (area)
pizza *pee-tsa*

Between two vowels **s** is pronounced *z*; everywhere else, it is pronounced *s*:

casa *kah-za* (house)
basta *bas-ta* (enough)
sono *son-oh* (I am)

E and **o** both have a weak and a strong pronunciation: the weak form is pronounced e as in 'pet'/o as in 'hot' and the strong form is pronounced *ay* as in 'pay'/*oh* as in 'go':

festa *fes-ta* (party)
borsa *bor-sa* (bag)
nero *nay-roh* (black)
calcio *kal-choh* (football)

Au is pronounced *ow* as in 'now':

auto *ow-toh* (car)

Getting started

bye	ciao *chow*
excuse me	mi scusi *mee skoo-zee*
good afternoon	buongiorno *bwon-jor-noh*
goodbye	arrivederci *arr-ee-vay-der-chee*
good evening	buonasera *bwon-a-say-ra*
good morning	buongiorno *bwon-jor-noh*
goodnight	buonanotte *bwon-a-not-tay*
hello, hi	ciao *chow*
no	no *noh*
OK	va bene *va bay-nay*
please	per favore *per fa-vor-ray*
thanks, thank you	grazie *grat-see-ay*
thanks very much	grazie mille *grat-see-ay meel-lay*
yes	sì *see*

I'd like ...
vorrei ...
vorr-ay-ee ...

we'd like ...
vorremmo ...
vorr-ay-moh ...

is there ...?
c'è ...?
chay ...?

are there ...?
ci sono ...?
chee son-oh ...?

where is ...?
dov'è ...?
doh-vay ...?

where are ...?
dove sono ...?
doh-vay son-oh ...?

how much is it?
quanto costa?
kwan-toh kos-ta?

do you speak English?
parla inglese?
par-la eeng-glay-zay?

Bare Essentials: Italian

how are you?
come stai?
kom-ay stah-ee?

fine, thanks
bene, grazie
bay-nay, grat-see-ay

what's your name?
come ti chiami?
kom-ay tee kee-ah-mee?

my name's …
mi chiamo …
mee kee-ah-moh …

where are you from?
di dove sei?
dee doh-vay say-ee?

I'm from …
sono di …
son-oh dee …

yes, please
sì, grazie
see, grat-see-ay

no, thanks
no, grazie
noh, grat-see-ay

thanks very much
grazie mille
grat-see-ay meel-lay

you're welcome
prego
pray-goh

see you later
ci vediamo
chee vay-dee-ah-moh

I'm sorry
mi dispiace
mee dees-pee-ah-chay

pardon?
(mi) scusi?
(mee) skoo-zee?

what?
come?
ko-may?

could you repeat that, please?
potrebbe ripetere, per favore?
po-treb-bay ree-pe-tay-ray, per fa-vor-ay?

how do you say … in Italian?
come si dice … in italiano?
ko-say see dee-chay … een ee-tal-yah-noh?

could you write it down for me?
me lo potrebbe scrivere?
*may loh po-**treb**-bay **skree**-vay-ray?*

I don't understand
non capisco
*non ka-**pees**-koh*

I love you
ti amo
*tee **ah**-moh*

shit!
merda!
mer-da!

Reading signs

aperto	open
attenzione	attention
chiuso	closed
divieto di sosta	no parking
donne	ladies *(toilet)*
fuori servizio	out of order
ingresso	entrance
prenotato	reserved
toilette	toilets
uomini	gents *(toilet)*
uscita	exit
vietato fumare	no smoking

Following directions

destra *des-tra* right
sempre dritto *sem-pray **dreet**-toh* straight on
sinistra *see-**nees**-tra* left

turn left/right
giri a sinistra/a destra
*jee-ree a see-**nees**-tra/a **des**-tra*

keep going straight on
vada sempre dritto
*vah-da **sem**-pray **dreet**-toh*

Language tips

- Italian has different ways of saying *you*: **tu**, **lei** and **voi**. Use tu when speaking to a friend or young person, and lei when speaking to an older person or stranger and in formal contexts. Voi is used when addressing more than one person (formally or informally). Note that the verb form will change accordingly. In this book we have used the tu form unless the context would make it inappropriate.
- Subject pronouns (*I, you, he* etc) are usually omitted in Italian unless needed for emphasis, as the verb ending shows which person is meant.
- All Italian nouns are either masculine (*m*) or feminine (*f*) in gender. As a general rule, those ending in **-o** are masculine and those ending in **-a** are feminine. Most plurals (though not all) can be formed by replacing a final **-o** by **-i** and a final **-a** by **-e**.
- The definite article (*the*) has different forms depending on the noun that follows it. So you will see **il**, **lo** or **l'** before masculine singular nouns and **i** or **gli** before masculine plurals; **la** or **l'** before feminine singular nouns and **le** before feminine plurals. The indefinite article (*a/an*) is **un** or **uno** before masculine singular nouns and **dei** or **degli** (*some*) before masculine plurals, **una** or **un'** before feminine singular nouns and **delle** before feminine plurals.

Numbers

0 zero *dze-roh*
1 uno *oo-noh*
2 due *doo-ay*

3 tre *tray*
4 quattro *kwat-troh*
5 cinque *cheeng-kway*

6 sei *say-ee*
7 sette *set-tay*
8 otto *ot-toh*
9 nove *noh-vay*
10 dieci *dee-ay-chee*
11 undici *oon-dee-chee*
12 dodici *doh-dee-chee*
13 tredici *tray-dee-chee*
14 quattordici *kwat-tor-dee-chee*
15 quindici *kween-dee-chee*
16 sedici *say-dee-chee*
17 diciassette *dee-chas-set-tay*
18 diciotto *dee-chot-toh*
19 diciannove *dee-cha-noh-vay*
20 venti *ven-tee*
21 ventuno *ven-too-noh*

22 ventidue *ven-tee-doo-ay*
30 trenta *tren-ta*
40 quaranta *kwa-ran-ta*
50 cinquanta *cheeng-kwan-ta*
60 sessanta *ses-san-ta*
70 settanta *set-tan-ta*
80 ottanta *ot-tan-ta*
90 novanta *noh-van-ta*
100 cento *chen-toh*
101 centouno *chen-toh-oo-noh*
500 cinquecento *cheeng-kway-chen-toh*
1000 mille *meel-lay*
1000000 un milione *oon mee-lyoh-nay*

Portuguese

Alphabet and pronunciation

The letters of the Portuguese alphabet are pronounced as follows:

a *ah*	**j** *zhoh-tUH*	**s** *ehs*
b *bay*	**k** *kah-pUH*	**t** *tay*
c *say*	**l** *ehl*	**u** *oo*
d *day*	**m** *ehm*	**v** *vay*
e *eh*	**n** *ehn*	**w** *double-yoo*
f *ehf*	**o** *o*	**x** *sheesh*
g *gay*	**p** *pay*	**y** *ee-gray-goo/eh-*
h *UH-gah*	**q** *kay*	*psee-lon*
i *ee*	**r** *ehRR*	**z** *zay*

Note the following transcriptions used in this book:

ah	as in 'bar'
ae	as in 'pay'
eh	as in 'pet'
ee	as in 'tree'
oh	as in 'home'
oo	as in 'spoon'

We have used the following codes to transcribe unfamiliar Portuguese sounds:

η   this indicates a nasal sound as in 'fine', 'pound', 'coin'. The nasalization shown by this symbol is always weaker than its preceding vowel, eg mãe *ma-eeη* (mother), pão *pouη* (bread), calções *cal-coiηs* (shorts)

zh   similar to the s in 'pleasure', eg: justo *zhoos-too* (just), jogar *zhoo-gar* (to play)

RR	similar to the *ch* in the Scottish word 'loch', although it can also be pronounced as a strongly rolled *r*, eg **carro** *kah-***RRoo** (car), **rato** **RRah**-*too* (mouse)
UH	similar to the *u* in 'cut', eg **para** *p***UH**-*r*UH (for), **cama** *k***UH**-*m*UH (bed)

Getting started

bye	adeus *UH*-**dae**-*oosh*, chau *chow*
excuse me	desculpe *desh*-**kool**-*p*, com licença *kom lee-***sain**-*sUH*
good afternoon	boa tarde *boh*-*UH* **tahr**-*d*
good evening	boa noite *boh*-*UH* **noy**-*t*
good morning	bom dia *bom* **dee**-*ya*
goodbye	adeus *UH*-**dae**-*oosh*
goodnight	boa noite *boh*-*UH* **noy**-*t*
hello, hi	olá *oh*-**lah**
no	não *noun*
OK	ok *oh*-**kay**
pardon	perdão *per*-**doun**
please	por favor *poohr* f*UH*-**vor**, se faz favor *s*-**fahsh** f*UH*-**vor**
thanks, thank you	obrigado (*said by man*)/obrigada (*said by woman*) *oh*-*bree*-**gah**-*doo*/*oh*-*bree*-**gah**-*dUH*
yes	sim *seen*

I'd like ...	**we'd like ...**
queria ...	queriamos ...
*ke-***ree**-*ya* ...	*ke-***ree**-*ya-moosh* ...

is there/are there...?	**where is ...?**
há ...?	onde é ...?
ah ...?	*on*-*d eh* ...?

where are ...?
onde fica ...?
on-d fee-kUH ...?

how much is it?
quanto custa?
kwUHn-too koosh-tUH?

do you speak English?
fala inglês?
fah-lUH een-glaysh?

how are you?
como está?
koh-moo esh-tah?

fine, thanks
bem, obrigado *(m)*/obrigada *(f)*
baim, oh-bree-gah-doo/oh-bree-gah-dUH

what's your name?
como se chama?
koh-moo se shUH-mUH?

my name's ...
chamo-me ...
shUH-moo mae ...

where are you from?
de onde é?
dae on-d eh?

I'm from ...
so dae ...
soh dae ...

yes, please
sim, se faz favor
seeɲ, s-fahsh fUH-vor

no, thanks
não, obrigado *(m)*/obrigada *(f)*
nouɲ, oh-bree-gah-doo/oh-bree-gah-dUH

thanks very much
muito obrigado *(m)*/obrigada *(f)*
mooy-too oh-bree-gah-doo/oh-bree-gah-dUH

you're welcome
de nada
dae nah-dUH

I'm sorry
desculpe
desh-kool-p

Bare Essentials: Portuguese

see you later
até logo
UH-teh loh-goo

I don't understand
não compreendo
nouŋ kom-pre-ain-doo

pardon?
perdão?
paer-douŋ?

what?
o quê?
oo kae?

could you repeat that, please?
importa-se de repetir?
eem-pohr-tUH-sae dae RRae-pae-teer?

how do you say ... in Portuguese?
como é que se diz ... em português?
koh-moo eh ke se deesh ... aim poohr-too-gaysh?

could you write it down for me?
importa-se de escrever?
eem-pohr-tUH-sae desh-kre-vehr?

I love you
amo-te
UH-moo-t

shit!
merda!
mehr-dUH!

Reading signs

aberto	open
atenção	attention
avariado	out of order
cuidado	attention
encerrado	closed
entrada	entrance
estacionamento prohibido	no parking
fechado	closed

fora de serviço	out of order
homens (H)	gents *(toilet)*
lababos	toilets
não fumadores	no smoking
reservado	reserved
saída	exit
senhoras (S)	ladies *(toilet)*

Following directions

à direita *ah dee-**ray**-tUH* right
à esquerda *ahsh-**kaer**-dUH* left
sempre em frente ***saim**-prae aim fraint* straight ahead

turn left/right
vire esquerda/ direita proibido
*veer ahsh-**kaer**-dUH/ah dee-**ray**-tUH*

keep going straight ahead
siga sempre em frente
*see-gUH **saim**-prae aim fraint*

> ### Language tips
>
> • Portuguese has different ways of saying *you*: **tu**, **você**, **vocês** and **os senhores/as senhoras** (*gentlemen/ladies*). Tu is only used when speaking informally to a good friend or younger person, while você is generally the word for 'you', especially with older people or in more formal situations. When addressing more than one person, use vocês in informal contexts and os senhores/as senhoras in formal ones. Note that the verb form will change accordingly. In this book we have used the more polite form, since that is what you will use until you really know somebody well.

- Subject pronouns (*I, you, he* etc) are usually omitted in Portuguese unless needed for emphasis, as the verb ending shows which person is meant.
- All Portuguese nouns are either masculine (*m*) or feminine (*f*) in gender. Most (but not all) nouns ending in **-o** are masculine and those ending in **-a** tend to be feminine. Most plurals are formed by adding either **-s** or **-es** to the singular noun.
- The definite article (*the*) for masculine nouns is **o** before singular nouns and **os** before plurals; in the feminine it is **a** before singular nouns and **as** before plurals. The indefinite article (*a/an*) before masculine nouns is **um** (singular)/**uns** (plural – *some*); before feminine nouns it is **uma** (singular)/**umas** (plural). Note that the article contracts when preceded by certain prepositions, so you may see words like **ao** (a + o), **do** (de + o), **da** (de + a), **no** (em + o), **na** (em + a), among others.
- Adjectives agree with the gender and number of the noun they describe and their endings may change accordingly.

Numbers

0 zero *zeh-roo*
1 um/uma *oom/oo-mUH*
2 dois/duas *doy-eesh/doo-UHsh*
3 três *traysh*
4 quatro *kwah-troo*
5 cinco *seen-koo*
6 seis *saysh*
7 sete *seh-t*
8 oito *oy-too*
9 nove *noh-v*
10 dez *deh-sh*
11 onze *on-z*

12 doze *do-z*
13 treze *trae-z*
14 catorze *kUH-tohr-z*
15 quinze *keen-z*
16 dezasseis *dae-zUH-saysh*
17 dezassete *dae-zUH-seh-t*
18 dezoito *dae-zoy-too*
19 dezanove *dae-zUH-noh-v*
20 vinte *veen-t*
21 vinte e um/uma *veen-t ee oom/oo-mUH*
22 vinte e dois/duas *veen-t ee*

doy-eesh/**doo**-UHsh
30 trinta *treen*-tUH
40 quarenta kwUH-**rain**-tUH
50 cinquenta seen-**kwain**-tUH
60 sessenta sae-**sain**-tUH
70 setenta sae-**tain**-tUH
80 oitenta oy-**tain**-tUH
90 noventa noo-**vain**-tUH

100 cem *sain*
101 cento e um/uma *sain*-too ee *oom*/oo-mUH
500 quinhentos/quinhentas keen-**yain**-toosh/keen-**yain**-tUHsh
1000 mil *meel*
1000 000 um milhão oom meel-youη

Spanish

In Spanish, words are pronounced as they are written, so once you master a few simple rules you will be able to read it correctly. Note that it is important to stress Spanish words correctly (the stressed syllables are shown in bold). There are regional variations, but here we give what might be called standard European Spanish, which is understood everywhere.

Alphabet and pronunciaton

The letters of the Spanish alphabet are pronounced as follows:

a *ah*	**j** *CHoh-ta*	**r** *err-ay*
b *bay*	**k** *kah*	**s** *ess-ay*
c *thay*	**l** *ell-ay*	**t** *tay*
d *day*	**m** *em-ay*	**u** *oo*
e *ay*	**n** *en-ay*	**v** *oo-bay*
f *ef-ay*	**ñ** *en-yay*	**w** *oo-bay dob-lay*
g *CHay*	**o** *oh*	**x** *ek-ees*
h *a-chay*	**p** *pay*	**y** *ee-gree-ay-ga*
i *ee*	**q** *koo*	**z** *thay-ta*

The following tips will help you to pronounce Spanish sounds correctly:

b, v these are pronounced in exactly the same way. At the start of a word, and after **m**, like *b* in 'beer'; elsewhere, the lips vibrate, but do not actually close to stop the flow of air

c before **a**, **o** and **u**, like *k* in 'king'; before **e** and **i**, like *th* in 'thing'

d at the start of a word, like *d* in 'dead'; elsewhere, like *th* in 'that'

g before **a**, **o** and **u**, like *g* in *gag*; before **e** and **i**, like *ch* in Scottish 'loch'. Note that in the combinations **gue** and **gui**, the **u** is silent unless written with a diaeresis (**ü**).

h always silent

j like *ch* in Scottish 'loch'

ll	similar to *lli* in 'million'
ñ	like *ny* in 'canyon'
qu	like *k* in 'king'
r	a lightly rolled *r* (tap your tongue once on the ridge behind your teeth)
rr	a strongly rolled *r*
v	see **b**, above
w	only found in loan words, pronounced like **b** above
z	like *th* in 'thing'

Note the following transcriptions used in this book:

ah as in 'bar'	*ee* as in 'tree'	*oh* as in 'go'	*ch* as in 'cheap'
air as in 'fair'	*eye* as in 'eye'	*oo* as in 'spoon'	*th* as in 'thin'
aw as in 'law'		*ow* as in 'town'	
ay as in 'pay'			

Some Spanish sounds do not exist in English and we have used the following codes to transcribe them:

| *CH* | as in Scottish 'loch' |
| *RR* | a strongly rolled *r* |

Getting started

bye	adiós *ad-yohs*
excuse me	perdone *pair-doh-nay*
good afternoon	buenas tardes *bway-nas tar-days*
goodbye	adiós *ad-yohs*
good evening	buenas tardes *bway-nas tar-days*
good morning	buenos días *bway-nos dee-as*
goodnight	buenas noches *bway-nas no-chays*
hello, hi	hola *oh-la*
no	no *noh*
OK	vale *bah-lay*

pardon ¿cómo? *ko-moh*
please por favor *por fa-bor*
thanks, thank you gracias *grath-yas*
yes sí *see*

I'd like ...
quería ...
kair-ee-ya ...

we'd like ...
queríamos ...
kair-ee-ya-mos ...

is there/are there ...?
¿hay ...?
eye ...?

how much is it?
¿cuánto es?
kwan-toh es?

where is ...?
¿dónde está...?
don-day es-ta ...?

where are ...?
¿dónde están ...?
don-day es-tan ...?

how are you?
¿cómo está?
ko-moh es-ta?

fine, thanks
bien, gracias
byen, grath-yas

what's your name?
¿cómo te llamas?
ko-moh tay yah-mas?

my name's ...
me llamo ...
may yah-moh ...

where are you from?
¿de dónde eres?
day don-day ay-res?

I'm from ...
soy de ...
soy day ...

yes, please
sí, por favor
see, por fa-bor

no, thanks
no, gracias
noh, grath-yas

thanks very much
muchas gracias
moo-chas grath-yas

you're welcome
de nada
day nah-da

see you later
hasta luego
as-ta lway-goh

I'm sorry
lo siento
loh syen-toh

pardon?
¿comó?
ko-moh?

what?
¿qué?
kay?

could you repeat that, please?
¿puedes repetir, por favor?
pway-des re-pe-teer, por fa-bor?

I don't understand
no entiendo
noh en-tyen-doh

how do you say ... in Spanish?
¿cómo se dice ... en español?
ko-moh say dee-thay ... en es-pan-yol?

could you write it down for me?
¿puedes escribírmelo?
pway-des es-kree-beer-may-loh?

do you speak English?
¿habla inglés?
ab-la eeng-glays?

I love you
te quiero
tay kyair-oh

shit!
mierda!
myair-da!

Reading signs

abierto	open
atención	attention
averiado	out of order
caballeros	gents' *(toilet)*
entrada	entrance
no ...	do not ...
prohibido aparcar	no parking
prohibido fumar	no smoking
reservado	reserved

salida	exit
señoras	ladies' *(toilet)*
servicios	toilets

Following directions

derecha *day-**rech**-a* right
izquierda *eeth-**kyair**-da* left
todo recto *toh-doh **rek**-toh* straight ahead

turn left/right
gire a la izquierda/a la derecha
*CHee-**ray** a la eeth-**kyair**-da/a la day-**rech**-a*

keep going straight on
sigue todo recto
*see-gay **toh**-doh **rek**-toh*

Language tips

- Spanish has different ways of saying *you*: **tú**, **usted**, **vosotros** and **ustedes**. Use tú when speaking to a friend, young person or someone you know well, and usted as a sign of respect when speaking to an older person or superior. When addressing more than one person, use vosotros in informal situations and ustedes in formal ones. Note that the verb form will change accordingly. In this book we have used the tú form unless the context would make inappropriate.
- Subject pronouns (*I, you, he* etc) are usually omitted in Spanish unless needed for emphasis, as the verb ending shows which person is meant.
- Spanish nouns are either masculine (*m*) or feminine (*f*) in gender. Often those ending in **-o** are masculine and those ending in **-a** are

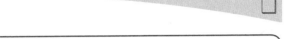

feminine, but there are exceptions. The definite article (*the*) is **el** before masculine singular nouns and **los** before masculine plurals; **la** before feminine singular nouns and **las** before feminine plurals. The indefinite article (*a/an*) for masculine nouns is **un** (singular)/**los** (plural – *some*); for feminine nouns it is **una** (singular)/**unas** (plural).

- Adjectives agree with the gender and number of the noun they describe and their endings may change accordingly.
- Note that in written Spanish, questions are preceded by an upside-down question mark (¿) as well as having a normal one at the end. The same applies to exclamations (¡).

Numbers

0 cero *thair-oh*	**18** dieciocho *dyeth-ee-och-oh*
1 uno *oo-noh*	**19** diecinueve *dyeth-ee-nway-bay*
2 dos *dos*	**20** veinte *bayn-tay*
3 tres *trays*	**21** veintiuno *bayn-tee-oo-noh*
4 cuatro *kwa-troh*	**22** veintidós *bayn-tee-dos*
5 cinco *theeng-koh*	**30** treinta *trayn-ta*
6 seis *seys*	**40** cuarenta *kwa-ren-ta*
7 siete *syet-ay*	**50** cincuenta *theeng-kwen-ta*
8 ocho *och-oh*	**60** sesenta *ses-en-ta*
9 nueve *nway-bay*	**70** setenta *set-en-ta*
10 diez *dyeth*	**80** ochenta *o-chen-ta*
11 once *on-thay*	**90** noventa *noh-ben-ta*
12 doce *doh-thay*	**100** cien *thyen*
13 trece *treth-ay*	**101** ciento uno *thyen-toh oo-noh*
14 catorce *ka-tor-thay*	**500** quinientos *keen-yen-tohs*
15 quince *keen-thay*	**1000** mil *meel*
16 dieciséis *dyeth-ee-seys*	**1000 000** un millón *oon meel-yohn*
17 diecisiete *dyeth-ee-syet-ay*	

Swedish

Alphabet and pronunciation

The Swedish alphabet has 29 letters which are pronounced as follows. Note that the additional letters **å**, **ä** and **ö** are placed at the end of the alphabet, so if you have a Swedish dictionary they will be found after z.

a *ah*	**k** *kor*	**u** *oo*
b *bee*	**l** *ell*	**v** *vee*
c *see*	**m** *emm*	**w** *doo-bell-vee*
d *dee*	**n** *enn*	**x** *ex*
e *ee*	**o** *oow*	**y** *yoe*
f *eff*	**p** *pee*	**z** *sair-ta*
g *yee*	**q** *koo*	**å** *aw* (as in "paw")
h *hor*	**r** *err*	**ä** *ai* (as in "air")
i *eeh*	**s** *ess*	**ö** *ur* (as in "burn")
j *gay*	**t** *tee*	

Consonants in Swedish are generally pronounced as in English, but note the following points:

s   always the like s in 'press' rather than in 'rose'

g   either hard as in 'guest', or like y in 'yes'; never as in 'gin'

j   like the y in 'yes', although there are a few exceptions where it is pronounced as in English.

You will only find **q**, **w** and **z** in foreign words, in which **w** is pronounced like v in 'vodka'.

With certain vowels, **k** and **sj** are pronounced like sh as in 'shoe'.

The word **och** (*and*) is pronounced like Scottish 'loch'. We have used the code *CH* to transcribe this sound.

Vowels are very important in the pronunciation of Swedish; note that long vowels are *very* long. The following transcriptions have been used to help you pronounce the vowels correctly:

a	as in 'back'	*e*	as in 'pet'	*i*	as in 'sip'
ah	as in 'bar'	*ee*	as in 'seen'	*o*	as in 'hot'
ai	as in 'air'	*eh*	as in 'tabouleh'	*oo*	as in 'cool'
aw	as in 'paw'	*ey*	as in 'hey'	*u*	as in 'push'
				ur	as in 'burn'

Getting started

bye	hejdå *hey-daw*
excuse me	ursäkta *oo-shek-ta*
goodbye	adjö *ad-yur*
good evening	godkväll *good-kvell*
good morning	godmorgon *good-mor-on*
goodnight	godnatt *good-natt*
hello, hi	hej *hey*
no	nej *ney*
OK	okey *o-key*
thanks, thank you	tack *tak*
yes	ja *yah*

I'd like ...
jag skulle vilja ...
*yahg **skool**-eh **vil**-ya ...*

we'd like ...
vi skulle vilja ...
*vee **skool**-eh **vil**-ya ...*

is there/are there ...?
finns det någon ...
*finns det **naw**-gon ...*

where is/are ...?
var är ...?
vahr airn ...?

how much is it?
hur mycket kostar det?
*hoor **muk**-eh **kost**-ar det?*

do you speak English?
pratar du engelska?
***prah**-tar doo **eng**-el-ska?*

what's your name?
vad heter du?
vahd hett-er doo?

my name's ...
jag heter ...
yahg hett-er ...

where are you from?
varifrån kommer du?
vahr-i-frawn komm-er doo?

I'm from ...
jag kommer från ...
yahg komm-er frawn ...

how are you?
hur mår du?
hoor maw doo?

fine, thanks
tack bra
tak brah

yes, please
ja tack
yah tak

no, thanks
nej tack
ney tak

thanks very much
tack så mycket
tak saw muk-eh

you're welcome
ingen orsak
ing-en or-shahk

see you later
vi ses snart
vee see-es snart

I'm sorry
jag är ledsen
yahg air led-sen

pardon?
förlåt?
fur-lawt?

what?
vadå?
va-daw?

could you repeat that, please?
kan du vara snäll och upprepa det?
kan doo vah-ra snell och oop-ree-pa det?

how do you say ... in Swedish?
hur säger man ... på svenska?
hoor say-er man ... paw sven-ska?

I don't understand
jag förstår inte
*yahg fursh-**taw** in-teh*

could you write it down for me?
kan du skriva det?
*kan doo **skree**-va det?*

I love you
jag älskar dig
*yahg **el**-ska day*

shit!
jävlar!
*yev-**lar**!*

Reading signs

damtoalett	ladies' *(toilet)*
herrtoalett	gents *(toilet)*
ingång	entrance
öppet	open
parkering förbjuden	no parking
reserverat	reserved
rökning förbjuden	no smoking
se upp	attention
stängt	closed
toalett	toilets
utgång	exit

Following directions

höger *hur*-ger right
rakt fram *rahkt fram* straight on
vänster *ven*-ster left

turn left/right
vänd till vänster/höger
*vend till **ven**-ster/**hur**-ger*

keep going straight on
kör rakt fram
shur rahkt fram

Language tips

- Swedish has two ways of saying *you*: **du**, used to address one person, and **ni**, used to address more than one. Ni can also be used to address one person very politely, but this is rare. In this book we have used du unless the context would make it inappropriate.
- All Swedish nouns belong to one of two genders, common or neuter. The indefinite article (*a/an*) is **en** before singular common nouns and **ett** before singular neuter (there is no indefinite article before plurals). The definite article (*the*) is tacked onto the end of the noun (**-en/-n** for common nouns, **-et/-t** for neuter): en båt (*a boat*) > båten, en blomma (*a flower*) > blomman; ett hus (*a house*) > huset, ett äpple (*an apple*) > äpplet.
- Forming plural nouns is more complicated as there is a range of possible ending. Indefinite plurals (eg *some cars*) are formed by adding a plural endings to the singular noun: en flicka (*a girl*) > flickor (*girls*), en pojke (*a boy*) > pojkar (*boys*), en student (*a student*) > studenter (*students*), ett äpple (*an apple*) > äpplen (*apples*). Definite plurals (eg *the cars*) are formed by taking the plural noun and adding the ending **-na**, **-a** or **-en**: flickor (*girls*) > flickorna (*the girls*), äpplen (*apples*) > äpplena (*the apples*), barn (*children*) > barnen.
- There is no word for *please* in Swedish: you normally just make your request and then add tack (*thank you*) at the end, eg kan jag få ... tack (*can I have ... thank you*). Alternatively, you can request something politely by starting your sentence with jag skulle vilja ... or jag skulle gärna ....

Numbers

0 noll *noll*	**18** arton *ahr-ton*
1 ett *et*	**19** nitton *ni-ton*
2 två *tvaw*	**20** tjugo *shoo-gi*
3 tre *tree*	**21** tjugoett *shoo-gi-ett*
4 fyra *fooy-ra*	**22** tjugotvå *shoo-gi-tvaw*
5 fem *fem*	**30** trettio *treh-tee-o*
6 sex *sex*	**40** fyrtio *fur-tee-o*
7 sju *shoo*	**50** femtio *fem-tee-o*
8 åtta *o-ta*	**60** sextio *sex-tee-o*
9 nio *nee-eh*	**70** sjuttio *shoo-tee-o*
10 tio *tee-eh*	**80** åttio *o-tee-o*
11 elva *el-va*	**90** nittio *ni-tee-o*
12 tolv *tolv*	**100** etthundra *ett-hoon-dra*
13 tretton *treh-ton*	**101** etthundraett *ett-hoon-dra-ett*
14 fjorton *fyoo-ton*	**500** femhundra *fem-hoon-dra*
15 femton *fem-ton*	**1000** ettusen *ett-toos-en*
16 sexton *sex-ton*	**1000 000** en miljon *en mil-yoon*
17 sjutton *shoo-ton*	

Bare Essentials: Swedish

Get the Party Started

Vital Vocab

to have a night out

Cz	jít večer někam ven	<u>yeet</u> **vech**-er **nyek**-am ven
Dan	at gå i byen	att gaw ee **bue**-uhn
Dut	uitgaan	**euit**-CHahn
Fr	sortir le soir	sor-**teer** luh swar
Ger	abends ausgehen	**ah**-buhnts **ows**-gay-uhn
Gr	βγαίνω έξω το βράδυ	**vye**-no **e**-xo to **vra**-thi
It	uscire una sera	oo-**shee**-ray **oo**-na **say**-ra
Por	sair à noite	s**UH**-eer ah **noy**-t
Sp	salir de noche	sa-**leer** day **no**-chay
Swe	att ha en helkväll	att hah en **hel**-kvel

to ask somebody out

Cz	pozvat někoho na večeři	**poz**-vat **nyek**-oho **na** vech-**erzh**-ee (literally: 'to invite somebody out to supper')
Dan	at invitere nogen ud	att in-vee-**ter**-uh **no**-wuhn ooTH
Dut	iemand uit vragen	**ee**-mant uit vrahCH-e(n)
Fr	inviter quelqu'un à sortir	AN-vee-tay kel-**kAN** a sor-**teer**
Ger	jemanden fragen ob er (m)/sie (f) ausgehen möchte	**yay**-man-duhm **frah**-guhn ob ehr/see **ows**-gay-uhn **meush**-tuh
Gr	ζητάω από κάποιον να βγούμε	zi-**ta**-o a-po ka-pi-on na **vghoo**-me
It	chiedere a qualcuno di uscire	kee-**ay**-de-ray a kwal-**koo**-noh dee oo-**shee**-ray
Por	convidar alguém para sair	kon-vee-**dahr** al-**gaim** p**UH**-rUH s**UH**-eer
Sp	invitar alguien a salir	een-bee-**tar** al-**gyen** a sa-**leer**
Swe	att bjuda ut någon	att **byoo**-da oot **naw**-gon

In the Know

As described in the *Drink Up!* and *Club Classics* chapters, European nightlife tends to go on quite late so there is less pressure to start early. If you're starting with a meal, times vary considerably depending on the country. In Scandinavia, Holland and the Czech Republic, people tend to have dinner early, around 6 or 7 pm, and the Germans not much later. In France and Portugal, you might go out for a meal about 8 pm; perhaps a bit later in Greece while in Spain it can easily be 10. In Italy, things tend to run much later in the centre and south than in the north. Spain, Italy and Greece in particular have a strong family culture, and you'll often see whole families going for an evening stroll and a drink with the kids in tow (children are welcome in restaurants and bars).

Scandinavians will often start the evening at someone's house, as drinks out are expensive: this is known in Sweden as a **förfest** or pre-party. Punctuality is important in Scandinavia and Germany – don't be more than 15 minutes late when meeting or visiting people, and let them know if you won't be on time. The Dutch are reasonably punctual too. In Greece, Spain and Italy, there is a more relaxed attitude and you shouldn't be surprised if you're kept waiting – nevertheless it's polite to let people know if you are running very late. The French are somewhere in between, but people often give a vague meeting time like 8-8.30. In Spain, Portugal and Greece it's more common to meet friends in a bar than at home; this is also popular among young Italians who often live with their parents into their twenties.

Greetings vary from country to country. Scandinavians, Germans and Czechs will usually just say hello, or perhaps shake hands when introduced to someone for the first time. However, the practice of greeting people with a kiss on the cheek is spreading, particularly among young women. Scandinavians tend to be good at introducing themselves to new people, so be prepared to do the same. In Greece, Spain, Portugal and Italy, people often greet each other with a kiss on each cheek (though two men would usually just shake hands). The French also kiss each other on the cheek (a practice known as **faire la bise**), but the number of kisses depends on the region: three is common, but some people give two and others four – just take your lead from the other person! Holland is similar: people generally give either one or three kisses, traditionally left, right, left. Don't mistake all this friendliness for flirtation – it's just part of the local culture!

Dating conventions are similar everywhere: it's common, but not essential, for a man to make the first move, while meeting through mutual friends remains one of the most popular ways of hooking up. The sexes are pretty much equal now, particularly in cities and among young people, although you may find things a little more traditional in Greece or Italy than in Holland, Germany or Scandinavia, where women tend to be very independent: for instance, they often insist on paying their share on a date (though most men still offer!). Like in the UK or US, typical first dates include meals or trips to the cinema, while arranging to meet for a coffee is a less formal option. In France and southern Europe it's quite common for girls and young women to be whistled at or approached by men in the street, so don't be alarmed if you experience this. Calling out **piropos** or flirtatious compliments to passing women is a Spanish tradition – these are similar in meaning to the cheesy chat-up lines in this book and should be taken about as seriously!

Smoking is still allowed (and popular) in pubs and clubs in most countries, though this may be changing: it's already banned in all public places in Sweden and Italy (some Italian premises have specially designated areas) with France and Germany set to follow suit, while a recent law in Spain states that larger premises must provide separate non-smoking areas. Swedish smokers needn't be put off by the cold: many places have provided them with shelters, outdoor heaters and even fleece blankets.

Listen up!

what are you doing tonight?

Cz	co děláš dneska večer?	*tso dyel-ash dnes-ka vech-er?*
Dan	hvad skal du lave i aften?	*va skal doo la-wuh ee aaf-tuhn?*
Dut	wat doe je vanavond?	*vat doo ye van-ah-vont?*
Fr	qu'est-ce que tu fais ce soir ?	*kess kuh tU fay suh swar?*
Ger	was machst du heute Abend?	*vas maCHst doo hoy-tuh ah-bunt?*
Gr	τι κάνεις σήμερα το βράδυ;	*ti ka-nis si-me-ra to vra-thi?*
It	cosa fai stasera?	*koh-za fah-ee sta-say-ra?*
Por	o que faz hoje à noite?	*oo kae fahsh ozh ah noy-t?*
Sp	¿qué haces esta noche?	*kay a-thes es-ta no-chay?*
Swe	vad gör du ikväll?	*vad yur doo i-kvell?*

why don't you come out with us?

Cz	nechceš s námi někam zajít?	*nyekh-tsesh s nam-ee nyek-am za-yeet?*
Dan	hvorfor tager du ikke med os?	*vor-for taar doo ik-kuh meTH oss?*
Dut	waarom ga je niet met ons uit?	*vahr-om CHah ye neet meht ons euit?*
Fr	tu devrais venir avec nous	*tU duh-vray vuh-neer a-vek noo*
Ger	warum kommst du nicht mit uns?	*va-rum komst doo nisht mit uns?*
Gr	γιατί δεν έρχεσαι μαζί μας;	*ya-ti then er-he-se ma-zi mas?*
It	perché non esci con noi?	*per-kay non esh-ee kon noh-ee?*
Por	porque não sai connosco?	*poor-kae noun sah-ee kon-nosh-koo?*
Sp	¿porqué no te vienes con nosotros?	*por-kay noh byen-es kon nos-ot-ros?*
Swe	vill du gå ut med oss?	*vill doo gaw oot med oss?*

would you like to go for a drink?

Cz	nezajdeme na drink?	*ne-zayd-em-e na dreenk?*
Dan	har du lyst til at gå ud og få en drink?	*haar doo luest til at gaw ooTH oe faw ehn drehnk?*

73

Dut	heb je zin om iets te gaan drinken? *hehp ye zin om eets te CHahn drink-e(n)?*
Fr	est-ce que tu veux aller boire un verre ? *ess kuh tU vuh a-lay bwar AN vair?*
Ger	hast du Lust, etwas trinken zu gehen? *hast doo lust, et-vas tring-kuhn tsoo gay-uhn?*
Gr	θάθελες να πάμε για ένα ποτό; *THa-THe-les na pa-me ya e-na po-to?*
It	ti va di andare a bere qualcosa? *tee va dee an-dah-ray a bay-ray kwal-koh-za?*
Por	quer ir beber um copo? *kehr eer bae-behr oom koh-poo?*
Sp	¿quieres salir a tomar algo? *kyair-es sa-leer a toh-mar al-goh?*
Swe	skulle du vilja gå på en drink? *skool-eh doo vil-ya gaw paw en drink?*

Fun facts!

If you want to stock up on booze in **Sweden**, you'll need to visit one of the state-run **Systembolaget** liquor stores. You also need to be at least 20.

In most countries the legal age for buying and drinking alcohol is 18; in **Holland** and **Germany** you can get beer and wine at 16 but must be 18 for spirits.

we could go to a club afterwards

Cz potom můžeme zajít někam do klubu *pot*-om *moozh*-e-me za-*yeet* do *kloob*-oo

Dan vi kan gå på diskotek bagefter *vee kan gaw paw dis-koh-***tehk** *ba-ef-tuhr*

Dut we kunnen daarna wel naar een disco gaan *ve* **ken**-e(n) *dahr-***nah** *vehl nahr en* **dis**-*koh CHahn*

Fr on pourrait aller en boîte après *ON poo-ray a-lay ON bwat a-pray*

Ger wir könnten hinterher in eine Disko gehen *veer* **keun**-*tuhn* **hin**-*tuh-hehr in* **ey**-*nuh* **dis**-*koh* **gay**-*un*

Gr μπορούμε να πάμε σ'ένα κέντρο μετά *bo-***roo**-*me na* **pa**-*me se-na* **ken**-*dro me-***ta**

It potremmo andare in discoteca dopo *po-***traym**-*moh an-***dah**-*ray een dees-koh-***tay**-*ka do-poh*

Por depois podíamos ir a uma discoteca *dae-***poy**-*eesh poo-***dee**-*UH-moosh eer UH oo-mUH deesh-koo-***teh**-*kUH*

Sp podemos ir a una discoteca luego *poh-***day**-*mos eer a oo-na dees-koh-***tay**-*ka* **lway**-*goh*

Swe vi kan gå på nattklubb efteråt *vee kan gaw paw* **natt**-*kloob ef-ter-awt*

would you like to come to a party tonight?

Cz nešel *(to man)*/nešla *(to woman)* bys dneska večer na party? *ne-shel/***nesh**-*la bees* **dnes**-*ka* **vech**-*er na part-ee?*

Dan vil du med til fest i aften? *vil doo meTH til fehst ee* **aaf**-*tuhn?*

Dut heb je zin om vanavond naar een feestje te komen? *hehp je zin om van-***ah**-*vont nahr en* **fayst**-*ye te* **kohm**-*e(n)?*

Fr est-ce que tu veux venir à une fête ce soir ? *ess kuh tU vuh vuh-neer a Un fet suh swar?*

Ger möchtest du heute Abend auf eine Party gehen? *meush*-*tuhst doo* **hoy**-*tuh* **ah**-*bunt owf* **ey**-*nuh* **par**-*ty* **gay**-*uhn?*

Gr θά θελες να έρθεις σ'ένα πάρτυ σήμερα το βράδυ; *THa-THe-les na* **er**-*THis se-na* **pa**-*rti* **si**-*me-ra to* **vra**-*thi?*

Get the Party Started

It	ti va di venire a una festa stasera? *tee va dee vay-**nee**-ray a oo-na fes-ta sta-**say**-ra?*
Por	quer ir a uma festa hoje à noite? *kehr eer UH oo-mUH fehsh-tUH ozh ah **noy**-t?*
Sp	¿quieres venir a una fiesta esta noche? *kyair-es ben-**eer** a oo-na **fyes**-ta **es**-ta no-chay?*
Swe	vill du komma på fest ikväll? *vill doo **kom**-er paw fest i-**kvell**?*

can I take you out tomorrow night?

Cz	můžu tě zítra večer pozvat na rande? *m**oozh**-oo tye **poz**-vat **zeet**-ra vech-er na rand-e?*
Dan	må jeg invitere dig ud i morgen aften? *maw yai in-vee-**ter**-uh dai ooTH ee morn **aaf**-tuhn?*
Dut	heb je zin om morgen met mij uit te gaan? *hehp ye zin om mor-CHe(n) meht may euit te CHahn?*
Fr	est-ce que je peux t'inviter à sortir demain soir ? *ess kuh zhuh puh tAN-vee-tay a sor-teer duh-mAN swar?*
Ger	wollen wir morgen Abend zusammen ausgehen? *vol-uhn veer mor-guhn ah-buhnt tsoo-zam-uhn ows-gay-uhn?*
Gr	θάθελες να βγούμε έξω αύριο βράδυ; *THa-He-les na **vghoo**-me e-xo **av**-ri-o **vra**-thi?*
It	usciresti con me domani sera? *oo-shee-**res**-tee kon may do-**mah**-nee **say**-ra?*
Por	quer sair comigo amanhã à noite? *kehr sUH-**eer** koo-**mee**-goo ah-mUHn-**yUH** ah **noy**-t?*
Sp	¿quieres salir conmigo mañana? *kyair-es sa-**leer** kon-**mee**-goh man-**yah**-na?*
Swe	vill du gå ut med mig imorgon? *vill doo gaw **oot** med may i-**mor**-on?*

76

Fun fact!

Spain is famous for its nightlife: listen out for the phrase **ir de marcha** (to go out partying), a national pastime from Thursday night right through the weekend!

Over to you

what is there to do at night here?

Cz	co se tady dá večer dělat?	*tso se **tad**-ee da **vech**-er **dyel**-at?*
Dan	hvad kan man lave her om aftenen?	*va kan man **la**-wuh hehr om **aaft**-nuhn?*
Dut	wat is er 's avonds te doen hier?	*vat is ehr **sah**-vonts te doon heer?*
Fr	qu'est ce qu'il y a à faire le soir ici ?	*kess keel ya a fair luh swar ee-see?*
Ger	was kann man hier abends machen?	*vas kan man heer **ah**-buh-nts ma-**CHuhn**?*
Gr	τι μπορείς να κάνεις εδώ το βράδυ;	*ti bo-**ris** na ka-nis e-**tho** to **vra**-thi?*
It	cosa si può fare qui di sera?	*koh-za see pwo **fah**-ray kwee dee **say**-ra?*

77

Por	o que há para fazer por aqui à noite? *oo kae ah **pUH**-rUH fUH-zaer poor UH-**kee** ah **noy**-t?*
Sp	¿qué se puede hacer por las noches aquí? *kay say **pway**-day a-**thair** por las **no**-chays a-**kee**?*
Swe	vad finns det att göra om kvällarna här? *vad finns det att **yur**-a om **kvell**-ar-na hair?*

I'll meet you at ... [*time*]

Cz	sejdeme se v ... *seyd-em-e se v ...*
Dan	lad os mødes klokken ... *lah oss **moeTH**-uhs **klok**-kuhn ...*
Dut	ik zie je om ... *ik zee ye om ...*
Fr	je te retrouverai à ... *zhuh tuh ruh-troo-vray a ...*
Ger	wir treffen uns um ... Uhr *veer **tref**-uhn uns um ... oor*
Gr	θα σε συναντήσω στις ... ώρα *THa se si-nan-**di**-so stis ... **o**-ra*
It	ci vediamo alle ... *chee vay-dee-**ah**-moh al-**lay** ...*
Por	encontramo-nos às ... *ain-kon-**trUH**-moo-noosh ahsh ...*
Sp	quedamos a las ... *kay-**dah**-mos a las ...*
Swe	vi kan träffas klockan ... *vee kan **tref**-as **klok**-an ...*

let's meet in/outside ... [*place*]

Cz	sejdeme se uvnitř/(venku) před ... *seyd-em-e se oov-nyeetrzh/(ven-koo) przhed ...*
Dan	lad os mødes i/ude foran ... *lah oss **moeTH**-uhs ee/ooTH-uh for-an ...*
Dut	laten we binnen/buiten ... afspreken *lah-te(n) ve bin-e(n)/beui-te(n) ... af-spray-ke(n)*
Fr	on pourrait se retrouver à/devant ... *ON poo-ray suh ruh-troo-vay a/duh-vON ...*
Ger	lass uns in/vor ... treffen *las uns in/for ... **tref**-uhn*
Gr	ας βρεθούμε μέσα/έξω ... *as vre-**THoo**-me me-sa/**e**-xo ...*
It	troviamoci dentro a/fuori da ... *troh-vee-**ah**-moh-chee **den**-troh a/foo-**oh**-ree da ...*
Por	encontramo-nos em/à entrada de ... *ain-kon-**trUH**-moo-noosh aim/ah ain-**trah**-dUH dae ...*

Sp	quedamos en/a la salida de ... *kay-**dah**-mos en/a la sa-**lee**-da day ...*
Swe	vi kan träffas inne på/utanför ... *vee kan **tref**-as **inn**-eh paw/**oot**-an-**fur** ...*

where is it?

Cz	kde to je? *kde to ye?*
Dan	hvor er det? *vor ehr deh?*
Dut	waar is het? *vahr is het?*
Fr	c'est où ? *say oo?*
Ger	wo ist das? *voh ist das?*
Gr	πού είναι; *poo i-ne?*
It	dov'è? *doh-**vay**?*
Por	onde é? *ond eh?*
Sp	¿dónde está? *don-day es-**ta**?*
Swe	var ligger det? *var **ligg**-er det?*

Get the Party Started

Fun fact!

Thursday night is typically 'student night' in **France**: it's a good time to find events and promotions aimed at young people, as well as to meet French students.

I'd love to

Cz	moc rád (m)/ráda (f) *mots r**a**d/r**a**d-a*
Dan	meget gerne *mai-yuht gern*

Dut	heel graag *hayl CHrahCH*
Fr	avec plaisir *a-vek play-zeer*
Ger	sehr gerne *zehr **gehr**-nuh*
Gr	πολύ θα τόθελα *po-**li** THa to-THe-la*
It	molto volentieri *mol-toh vol-en-tee-**ay**-ree*
Por	com prazer *kom prUH-zaer*
Sp	me encantaría *may eng-kan-ta-**ree**-a*
Swe	gärna *yair-na*

thanks, but we already have plans

Cz	díky, ale už něco máme *deek-ee, al-e oozh nyet-so mam-e*
Dan	tak, men vi har allerede lavet planer *tahk, mehn vee haar al-luh-reTH-uh la-wuht plah-nuhr*
Dut	dank je, maar we hebben al andere plannen *dank ye, mahr ve hehb-e(n) al an-der-e plan-e(n)*
Fr	merci, mais on a déjà quelque chose de prévu *mair-see, may on a day-zha kel-kuh shohz duh pray-vU*
Ger	danke, aber wir haben schon etwas vor *dang-kuh, ah-buh veer hah-buhn shohn et-vas for*
Gr	ευχαριστώ, αλλά έχουμε ήδη κανονίσει *ef-ha-ri-sto, a-la e-hoo-me i-thi ka-no-ni-si*
It	grazie, ma abbiamo già previsto qualcosa *grat-see-ay, ma ab-bee-ah-moh ja pray-vees-toh kwal-koh-za*
Por	obrigado (m)/obrigada (f), mas já temos planos *oh-bree-gah-doo/oh-bree-gah-dUH, mUHsh zhah tae-moosh plUH-noosh*
Sp	gracias, pero ya temenos planes *grath-yas, pe-roh ya te-nay-mos plah-nays*
Swe	tack, men vi har redan andra planer *tak, men vee hahr reh-dan and-ra plahn-er*

I'll meet you a bit later

| Cz | sejdeme se o něco později/o trochu později *seyd-em-e se o nyets-o pozd-yey-ee/o trokh-oo pozd-yey-ee* |
| Dan | lad os mødes lidt senere *lah oss moeTH-uhs litt sehn-uhr* |

Dut	ik zie je straks *ik zee ye straks*
Fr	je te retrouverai un peu plus tard *zhuh tuh ruh-troo-vray AN puh plU tar*
Ger	wir treffen uns etwas später *veer tref-uhn uns et-vas shpeh-tuh*
Gr	θα σε συναντήσω λίγο αργότερα *THa se si-nan-di-so li-gho ar-gho-te-ra*
It	ci vediamo un po' più tardi *chee vay-dee-ah-moh oon po pyoo tar-dee*
Por	encontramo-nos mais tarde *ain-kon-trUH-moo-noosh mah-eesh tahr-d*
Sp	quedamos un poco más tarde *kay-dah-mos oon poh-koh mas tar-day*
Swe	jag kommer lite senare *yahg kom-er lee-teh sen-ahr-eh*

can I take your number?

Cz	můžu si vzít tvoje číslo? *moozh-oo see vzeet tvoy-e chees-lo?*
Dan	må jeg få dit nummer? *maw yai faw ditt noe-muhr?*
Dut	mag ik je nummer? *maCH ik ye nem-er?*
Fr	est-ce que je peux avoir ton numéro ? *ess kuh zhuh puh a-vwar tON nU-may-roh?*
Ger	darf ich deine Nummer haben? *darf ish dey-nuh num-uh hah-buhn?*
Gr	μπορείς να μου δώσεις το τηλέφωνό σου; *bo-ris na moo tho-sis to ti-le-fo-no soo?*
It	mi daresti il tuo numero? *mee da-res-tee eel too-oh noo-may-roh?*
Por	dá-me o seu número? *dah-mae oo say-oo noo-mae-roo?*
Sp	¿me das tu teléfono? *may das too te-lay-fon-oh?*
Swe	får jag ditt nummer? *faw yahg dit numm-er?*

here's my mobile number

| Cz | tady je moje číslo (na mobil) *tad-ee ye moy-e chees-lo (na mob-eel)* |
| Dan | her er nummeret til min mobiltelefon *hehr ehr noe-muhrt til meen mob-eel-te-luh-fon* |

Dut dit is mijn mobiele nummer *dit is mayn mob-eel-e nem-er*

Fr voici mon numéro de portable *wa-see mON nU-may-roh duh por-tahbl*

Ger hier ist meine Handynummer *heer ist mey-nuh hen-dee-num-uh*

Gr αυτό είναι το κινητό μου *af-to i-ne to ki-ni-to moo*

It questo è il mio numero di cellulare *kwes-toh ay eel mee-oh noo-may-roh dee chel-loo-lah-ray*

Por este é o meu número de telemóvel *aesh-t eh oo may-oo noo-mae-roo dae teh-leh-moh-vehl*

Sp te doy (el número de) mi móvil *tay doy (el noo-mair-oh day) mee mob-eel*

Swe det här är mitt mobilnummer *det hair air mitt mob-eel-numm-er*

I'll call/text you later

Cz potom ti zavolám/pošlu esemesku *pot-om tee za-vol-am/posh-loo es-em-es-koo*

Dan jeg ringer/sender dig en sms senere *yai rehng-uhr/sen-nuhr dai ehn ehs-ehm-ehs sehn-uhr*

Dut ik bel/sms je later *ik behl/ehs-ehm-ehs ye lah-ter*

Fr je t'appelle/t'envoie un texto plus tard *zhuh ta-pell/tON-vwa AN tek-stoh plU tar*

Ger ich rufe/simse dich später an *ish roo-fuh/sim-zuh dish shpeh-tuh an*

Gr θα σε πάρω/στείλω μήνυμα αργότερα *THa se pa-ro/sti-lo mi-ni-ma ar-gho-te-ra*

It ti chiamo/mando un SMS più tardi *tee kee-ah-moh/man-doh oon ess-ay-em-may-ess-ay pyoo tar-dee*

Por telefono-lhe/envio-lhe uma mensagem mais tarde *tae-lae-foh-noo-lyee/ain-vee-oo-lyee oo-mUH main-sah-zhaim mah-eesh tahr-d*

Sp luego te llamo/te mando un mensaje *lway-goh tay ya-moh/tay man-doh oon men-sa-CHay*

Swe jag ringer/textar dig senare *yahg ring-er/text-ar day sen-ahr-eh*

see you later!

Cz	zatím ahoj!	*za-teem a-hoy!*
Dan	vi ses senere!	*vee sehs sen-uhr!*
Dut	tot later!	*tot lah-ter!*
Fr	à plus tard !	*a plU tar!*
Ger	bis später!	*bis shpeh-tuh!*
Gr	τα λέμε αργότερα!	*ta le-me ar-gho-te-ra!*
It	a dopo!	*a do-poh!*
Por	até logo!	*UH-teh loh-goo!*
Sp	¡hasta luego!	*as-ta lway-goh!*
Swe	hej så länge!	*hey saw leng-eh!*

sorry I'm late

Cz	promiň, že jdu pozdě	*pro-meeny, zhe ydoo poz-dye*
Dan	undskyld, jeg kommer for sent	*uhn-skuel, yai kom-muhr for sehnt*
Dut	sorry dat ik te laat ben	*sor-ree dat ik te laht behn*
Fr	désolé d'être en retard	*day-zoh-lay detr ON ruh-tar*
Ger	entschuldige die Verspätung	*ent-shul-di-guh dee fehr-shpeh-tung*
Gr	συγνώμη που άργησα	*sigh-no-mi poo ar-ghi-sa*
It	mi dispiace, sono in ritardo	*mee dees-pee-ah-chay, son-oh een ree-tar-doh*
Por	desculpe o atraso	*desh-kool-p oo UH-trah-zoo*
Sp	siento llegar tarde	*syen-toh yay-gar tar-day*
Swe	ledsen att jag är sen	*led-sen att yahg air sehn*

♥ The Language of Love ♥

I seem to have lost my phone number, can I borrow yours?

Cz myslím, že jsem ztratil *(m)*/ztratila *(f)* svoje číslo, můžu si půjčit tvoje?
*mees-leem, zhe ysem **ztrat**-eel/**ztrat**-eel-a **svoy**-e **chees**-lo, **moozh**-oo see **pooy**-cheet **tvoy**-e?*

Dan jeg har tabt nummeret til min mobiltelefon, må jeg låne dit?
*yai haar taapt **noe**-muhrt til meen mo-**beel**-te-luh-fon, maw yai **lawn**-uh deet?*

Dut ik ben mijn telefoonnummer verloren, mag ik de jouwe lenen?
*ik behn mayn tay-le-**foon-nem**-er fer-**lor**-e(n), maCH ik de **yow**-e **layn**-e(n)?*

Fr je crois que j'ai perdu mon numéro de téléphone, est-ce que je peux t'emprunter le tien?
zhuh krwa kuh zhay pair-dU mON nU-may-roh duh tel-ay-fon, ess kuh zhuh puh tON-pruhn-tay luh tyAN?

Ger ich glaube, ich hab meine Telefonnummer verloren, darf ich mir vielleicht deine leihen?
*ish **glow**-buh, ish hahb **mey**-nuh te-le-**fohn**-num-uh fehr-**lor**-uhn, darf ish meer vee-**leyCHt dey**-nuh **ley**-uhn?*

Gr μου φαίνεται ότι έχασα το νούμερό μου, μπορώ να δανειστώ το δικό σου;
*moo **fe**-ne-te **o**-ti **e**-ha-sa to **noo**-me-ro moo, bo-**ro** na tha-ni-**sto** to thi-**ko** soo?*

It mi sa che ho perso il mio numero di telefono, mi daresti mica il tuo?

*mee sa kay oh **per**-soh eel **mee**-oh **noo**-may-roh dee tay-**lef**-o-noh, mee da-**res**-tee **mee**-ka eel **too**-oh?*

Por perdi o meu número de telefone, empresta-me o seu?

*paer-**dee** oo **may**-oo **noo**-mae-roo dae tae-lae-**fon**, aim-**prehsh**-tUH-mae oo **say**-oo?*

Sp creo que he perdido mi número de móvil, ¿me prestas el tuyo?

***kray**-oh kay hay pair-**dee**-doh mee **noo**-mair-oh day **mob**-eel, may **pres**-tas el **too**-yoh?*

Swe jag tycks ha förlorat mitt mobilnummer, kan jag låna ditt?

*yahg tuks hah fur-**lor**-at mit mob-**eel**-numm-er, kan yahg **law**-na dit?*

Drink Up! 🍸

Vital vocab

bar

Cz	bar	*bar*
Dan	bar	*bah*
Dut	bar	*bar*
Fr	bar	*bar*
Ger	Bar	*bah*
Gr	μπαρ	*bar*
It	(american) bar	*(a-**may**-ree-kan) bar*
Por	bar	*bahr*
Sp	bar	*bar*
Swe	bar	*bahr*

to go for a drink

Cz	jít na skleničku/na drink	*yeet na sklen-eech-koo/na dreenk*
Dan	at gå ud og tage en drink	*att gaw ooTH oe tah ehn drehnk*
Dut	iets gaan drinken	*eets CHahn **drink**-e(n)*
Fr	aller boire un verre	*a-lay bwar AN vair*
Ger	etwas trinken gehen	*et-vas **tring**-kuhn **gay**-uhn*
Gr	πάω για ένα ποτό	*pa-o ya **e**-na po-**to***
It	andare a bere qualcosa	*an-**dah**-ray a **bay**-ray kwal-**koh**-za*
Por	ir tomar um copo	*eer too-**mar** oom **koh**-poo*
Sp	ir a tomar algo	*eer a toh-**mar** al-goh*
Swe	gå ut på en drink	*gaw oot paw en drink*

In the Know

In most European countries, going out for a few drinks is a sociable yet relatively civilized affair: people spread their drinking over the course of a long evening and you tend not to see rowdy groups of drunk locals in the streets (particularly not women). In countries such as France, Italy and Greece, drunkenness is frowned upon – people go out to dance or chat rather than to drink as much as they can. Attitudes are more liberal in Sweden and Denmark, where it's more common for young people to get drunk. Opening hours tend to be longer than in Britain – bars close between 1 and 3 am depending on the country and the size of the town – so people go out a bit later, around 8 or 9 pm (later in southern Europe).

In most places table service is the norm in pubs (but beware in Denmark, where it usually indicates an expensive venue!). In Germany, Holland and the Czech Republic people generally stay in one place till closing time, though pub crawls are not unheard of (known in Germany as a **Kneipenbummel**). It's usual to pay for your own drinks individually – if you want to buy rounds, ask your friends if they're happy with this. In Portugal, Spain and Greece people often spend the evening bar-hopping, having a small drink in each place and paying when they leave. Greeks like to start the evening off in their local or **steki**, where everyone knows each other. A traditional Greek **taverna** is a good place to start, and to meet people: they are relaxed places serving food and drinks and are open till late. In Scandinavia, the high price of alcohol means young people often start the evening off at someone's house. Although Sweden is famous for its schnapps and vodka, beer and cider are generally the cheapest options – **storstark**, meaning 'big-strong', is a popular type of beer.

In Spain, it's common to have some nibbles or finger-food (**tapas**) with your drink, while in Greece you usually get some nuts or crisps – snacks are particularly generous in the north. In Germany, food depends on the

Drink Up!

type of establishment: a **Bar** or **Kneipe** is basically a pub (which may serve a few nibbles), a **Café** serves hot drinks and cakes as well as alcohol, and a **Gaststätte** is a sort of bistro/small restaurant where you can also go for a drink (slightly smarter than the other places). Some French bars serve snacks, but hungry drinkers often just pop out to the nearest sandwich or kebab shop and bring something back. Swedish pubs usually have a few snacks available: if you want a change from crisps and olives, how about some reindeer sausage with your pint?

Names can be confusing: in Portugal, 'bars' tend to be more upmarket, trendy places – for cheaper drinks and a bite to eat, try a 'café' (open till late). In Italy, a 'bar' is more like what we call a café, only open during the day and serving coffee and light food. *Our* idea of a bar is called an **american bar** in Italy; alternatives are a **birrerie** (pub), a **discopub** (bar with a dancefloor; a bit trendier) or a **live music club** (bar with live music). Holland is famous for its **coffeeshops** which sell marijuana as well as drinks – if you're just looking for some innocent refreshments, make sure you go to a **café** instead!

Beer is probably the most popular (and cheapest) drink everywhere, though wine is usually available (mainly local vintages if you're in a wine-growing area) as are local speciality drinks and, increasingly, alcopops. Spirits tend to be more expensive, but be warned that measures are generally far more generous than British ones (particularly in southern Europe)!

Listen up!

what would you like to drink?

Cz   co si dáte k pití? *tso see **dat**-e k **peet**-ee?*
Dan   hvad vil du have at drikke? *vaTH vil doo hah att **dre**-kuh?*
Dut   wat wilt u drinken? *vat vilt oo **drink**-e(n)?*
Fr   qu'est-ce que vous voulez boire ? *kess kuh voo voo-lay bwar?*

Ger	was möchten Sie trinken? *vas meush-tuhn zee tring-kuhn?*
Gr	τι θα θέλατε να πιείτε; *ti THa THe-la-te na pi-i-te?*
It	cosa prendete da bere? *koh-za pren-day-tay da bay-ray?*
Por	o que vai beber? *oo kae va-ee bae-baer?*
Sp	¿qué quieres de beber? *kay kyair-es day be-bair?*
Swe	vad vill ni ha att dricka? *vahd vill nee hah at dri-ka?*

can I ask you to pay now, please?

Cz	můžu vás požádat o zaplacení? *moozh-oo vas po-zha-dat o za-plat-se-nee?*
Dan	må jeg bede dig om at betale nu? *maw yai bey dai om att be-tah-luh noo?*
Dut	zou u kunnen betalen, alstublieft? *zow oo ken-en be-tahl-e(n), als-too-bleeft?*
Fr	je peux encaisser, s'il vous plaît ? *zhuh puh ON-kess-ay, seel voo play?*
Ger	könnte ich bitte kassieren? *keun-tuh ish bit-uh kas-eer-uhn?*
Gr	θα μπορούσατε να με πληρώσετε τώρα, παρακαλώ; *THa bo-roo-sa-te na me pli-ro-se-te to-ra, pa-ra-ka-lo?*
It	le dispiacerebbe pagare ora, per favore? *lay dees-pee-ah-cher-eb-bay pa-gah-ray o-ra, per fa-vor-ay?*
Por	importa-se de pagar agora, se faz favor? *eem-pohr-tUH-sae dae pa-gahr UH-gohr-UH, s-fahsh fUH-vor?*
Sp	¿puede pagar ahora, por favor? *pway-day pa-gar a-or-a, por fa-bor?*
Swe	får jag be er betala? *faw yahg ber er be-tah-la?*

I'm sorry, you can't smoke here

Cz	promiňte, tady nemůžete kouřit *pro-meenyte, tad-ee ne-moozh-ete ko-oorzh-eet*
Dan	du må desværre ikke ryge her *doo maw des-vehr-uh ik-kuh rue-uh hehr*
Dut	het spijt me, maar u mag hier niet roken *het spayt me, mahr oo maCH heer neet roh-ke(n)*

Drink Up!

89

Fr	je suis désolé mais il est interdit de fumer ici *zhuh swee day-zoh-lay may eel et AN-tair-dee de fU-may ee-see*
Ger	tut mir leid, rauchen ist hier nicht erlaubt *toot meer leyt, row-CHuhn ist heer nisht ehr-lowpt*
Gr	συγνώμη, δεν μπορείτε να καπνίσετε εδώ *si-ghno-mi, then bo-ri-te na ka-pni-se-te e-tho*
It	mi dispiace, qui non si può fumare *mee dees-pee-ah-chay, kwee non see pwo foo-mah-ray*
Por	desculpe, mas não pode fumar aqui *desh-kool-p, mUHsh nouŋ pod foo-mahr UH-kee*
Sp	lo siento, no se puede fumar aquí *loh syen-toh, noh say pway-day foo-mar a-kee*
Swe	tyvärr får ni inte röka här *too-vair faw nee in-teh rur-ka hair*

Fun fact!

Beer is **Germany**'s national drink, and there are plenty to try. In Bavaria, it's said that as long as you can hold a full **Maßkrug** (one-litre tankard) steady at arm's length, you're not drunk! Don't forget Germany also makes some excellent wines, if beer's not your tipple.

Over to you

where are the best bars?

| Cz | kde jsou nejlepší bary? *kde yso-oo ney-lep-shee bar-ee?* |

Dan	hvor er de bedste barer? *vor ehr dee **bes**-tuh **bah**-uh?*
Dut	waar zijn de beste café's? *vahr zayn de **best**-e ka-**fays**?*
Fr	où sont les meilleurs bars ? *oo sON lay may-uhr bar?*
Ger	wo sind die besten Kneipen? *voh zint dee **bes**-tuhn **kney**-puhn?*
Gr	πού είναι τα καλύτερα μπαρ; *poo i-ne ta ka-li-te-ra bar?*
It	dove sono i migliori locali? *doh-vay so-noh ee mee-**lyoh**-ree lo-kah-lee?*
Por	onde são os melhores bares? *ond souŋ oosh mel-**yoh**-raesh bah-raesh?*
Sp	¿dónde están los mejores bares? *don-day es-**tan** los me-**CHor**-ays bar-ays?*
Swe	var finns de bästa barerna? *vahr finns dom **bes**-ta **bahr**-er-na?*

where do the locals hang out?

Cz	kam chodí místní? *kam khod-ee meest-nee?*
Dan	hvor hænger de lokale ud? *vor **hehng**-uh dee loh-**kah**-luh ooTH?*
Dut	waar gaan de Nederlanders naar toe? *vahr CHahn de **nayd**-er-land-ers nahr too?*
Fr	quels sont les bars que fréquentent les gens du coin ? *kel sON lay bar kuh fray-kONt lay zhON dU kwAN?*
Ger	wo gehen die Einheimischen am liebsten hin? *voh **gay**-uhn dee **eyn**-hey-mish-uhn am **leeb**-stuhn hin?*
Gr	πού πάνε οι ντόπιοι; *poo pa-ne i do-pi-i?*
It	dove va di solito la gente del posto? *doh-vay va dee so-lee-toh la jen-tay del pos-toh?*
Por	que locais é que as pessoas daqui frequentam? *kae loo-**kah**-eesh eh kae UHsh pae-**soh**-UHsh dUH-kee frae-**kwain**-touŋ?*
Sp	¿por dónde se mueve la gente de aquí? *por **don**-day say **mway**-bay la **CHen**-tay day a-kee?*
Swe	vart brukar lokalinvånarna gå? *vart **broo**-kar lo-**kahl**-in-**vaw**-nar-na gaw?*

Drink Up!

Fun fact!

The ancient **Greeks** always drank their wine watered down – drinking it neat was considered barbaric, so you might want to take it easy!

what time do the pubs shut around here?

Cz	v kolik hodin tady zavírají hospody? *v kol-eek hod-een tad-ee za-veer-ay-ee hos-pod-ee?*
Dan	hvornår lukker barerne her i nærheden? *vor-naw luh-kuh bah-nuh hehr ee nehr-heTH-uhn?*
Dut	hoe laat sluiten de café's hier? *hoo laht sleuit-e(n) de ka-fays heer?*
Fr	à quelle heure ferment les bars dans le coin ? *a kel uhr fairm lay bar dON luh kwAN?*
Ger	wann schließen die Kneipen hier? *van schlee-suhn dee kney-puhn heer?*
Gr	τι ώρα κλείνουν τα μπαρ εδώ; *ti o-ra kli-noon ta bar e-tho?*
It	a che ora chiudono le birrerie qui? *a kay o-ra kyoo-do-noh lay beer-ray-ree-ay kwee?*
Por	a que horas é que fecham os bares aqui? *UH kae ohr-UHsh eh kae fehsh-oun oosh bah-raesh UH-kee?*
Sp	¿a qué hora cierran aquí los bares? *a kay or-a thyaiRR-an a-kee los bar-ays?*
Swe	vilken tid stänger pubarna här? *vil-ken teed steng-ar poob-ar-na hair?*

we're looking for somewhere lively/fairly quiet

Cz hledáme něco, kde to žije/něco tiššího *hled-a-me nyet-so, kde to zhee-ye/nyet-so teesh-ee-ho*

Dan vi leder efter et sted med gang i/et mere roligt sted *vee leTH-uhr eft-uhr eht stehTH meTH gahng ee/eht mehr roh-litt steTH*

Dut we zijn op zoek naar iets levendigs/rustigs *ve zayn op zook nahr eets lay-ven-degs/rest-egs*

Fr on cherche un endroit animé/un peu tranquille *ON shairsh ANn ON-drwa a-nee-may/AN puh trON-keel*

Ger wir suchen etwas lebhaftes/eher ruhiges *veer zoo-CHuhn et-vas layb-haf-tuhs/ay-uh roo-ig-uhs*

Gr ψάχνουμε για κάτι έντονο/ήσυχο *psa-hnoo-me ya ka-ti en-do-no/i-si-ho*

It stiamo cercando un posto animato/un po' tranquillo *stee-ah-moh cher-kan-doh oon pos-toh an-ee-mah-toh/oon po tran-kweel-loh*

Por queremos ir a um local animado/sossegado *kae-ray-moosh eer UH oom loo-kahl UHn-ee-mah-doo/soo-sgah-doo*

Sp estamos buscando un lugar con marcha/un lugar tranquilo *es-tah-mos boos-kan-doh oon loo-gar kon mar-cha/oon loo-gar trang-kee-loh*

Swe vi söker ett livligt/ganska lugnt ställe *vee sur-ker ett leev-ligt/gan-ska loongt stel-eh*

I'll have a beer/a gin and tonic/a rum and Coke®

Cz dám si pivo/gin s tonikem/kolu s rumem *dam see pee-vo/dzheen s ton-ee-kem/kol-oo s room-em*

Dan jeg vil gerne have en øl/en gin og tonic/en rum og cola *yai vil ger-nuh hah ehn eul/ehn gin oe ton-ik/ehn rum oe ko-la*

Dut een biertje/een gin en tonic/een rum en cola, graag *en beer-tye/en jin en ton-ik/en rem en koh-la, CHrahCH*

Fr je vais prendre une bière/un gin-tonic/un rhum-coca *zhuh vay prONdr Un byair/AN jeen-ton-eek/AN rom-koh-ka*

Ger   für mich ein Bier/einen Gin/einmal Rum-Cola *fuur mish eyn beer/eyn-uhn jinn/eyn-mahl rum-koh-la*

Gr   θα πάρω μία μπύρα/ενα τζιν με τόνικ/ένα ρούμι με κόκα κόλα *THa pa-ro mi-a bi-ra/e-na tzin me to-nik/e-na roo-mi me ko-ka ko-la*

It   prendo una birra/un gin and tonic/una coca e rum *pren-doh oo-na beer-ra/oon jeen an to-neek/oo-na koh-ka ay room*

Por   quero uma cerveja/um gin tónico/um rum com coca-cola *keh-roo oo-mUH saer-vay-zhUH/oom jeeη toh-nee-koo/oom room kom koh-kUH-koh-lUH*

Sp   una cerveza/un gin-tonic/un ron con cola-cola *oo-na thair-bay-tha/oon jeen-ton-eek/oon ron kon koh-ka koh-la*

Swe   jag tar en öl/en gin och tonic/en rom och cola *yahg tahr en url/en yin oCH to-nik/en rom ochCH ko-la*

Drink Up!

Fun fact!

The **Danes** love their beer so much that they make special brews for different times of year. The annual launch of Tuborg's strong **Julebryg** (Christmas beer) is an eagerly anticipated event, heralded by posters announcing that the first snow will fall at exactly 20:59 on the first Friday of November (known as **J-Day**)!

a glass of white/red wine, please

Cz   skleničku bílého/červeného vína, prosím *sklen-eech-koo **beel**-e-ho/**cher**-ven-eho **veen**-a, pro-**seem***

Dan et glas hvidvin/rødvin, tak *eht glass **viTH**-veen/**roeTH**-veen, tahk*

Dut een glas witte/rode wijn, alsjeblieft *en CHlas **vit**-e/**rohd**-e vayn, als-ye-**bleeft***

Fr   un verre de vin blanc/rouge, s'il vous plaît *AN vair duh vAN blONg/roozh, seel voo play*

Ger ein Glas Weißwein/Rotwein bitte *eyn glahs **veys**-veyn/**roht**-veyn **bit**-uh*

Gr   ένα ποτήρι άσπρο/κόκινο κρασί, παρακαλώ *e-na po-**ti**-ri a-spro/**ko**-ki-no kra-**si**, pa-ra-ka-**lo***

It   un bicchiere di vino bianco/rosso, per favore *oon beek-kee-**ay**-ray dee **vee**-noh **byan**-koh/**ros**-soh, per fa-**vor**-ay*

Por um copo de vinho branco/tinto, se faz favor *oom **koh**-poo dae **veen**-yoo brUHn-koo/**teen**-too, s-**fahsh** fUH-**vor***

Sp   un blanco/un tinto, por favor *oon **blang**-koh/oon **teen**-toh, por fa-**bor***

Swe ett glas vitt vin/rött vin, tack *ett glahs veet vin/rurt vin, tack*

do you do cocktails?

Cz   děláte koktejly? *dye-**la**te **kok**-teyl-ee?*

Dan serverer I cocktails? *sehr-**vehr**-uh ee **kok**-tails?*

Dut hebben jullie cocktails? *hehb-e(n) **jel**-lee **kok**-tayls?*

Fr   est-ce que vous faites des cocktails ? *ess kuh voo fet day kok-tel?*

Ger haben Sie auch Cocktails im Angebot? *hah-buhn zee owCH **kok**-taylz im **ang**-guh-boht?*

Gr   φτιάχνετε κοκτέιλ; *ftia-hne-te ko-**kte**-il?*

It   fate dei cocktail? *fah-tay day-ee **kok**-tail?*

Por servem cocktails? *sehr-vaim kok-tUH-eesh?*

Sp   ¿hacen cócteles? *a-then **kok**-tel-ays?*

Swe serverar ni cocktails? *ser-**veer**-ahr nee **kok**-tails?*

no thanks, I don't drink

Cz ne, díky, nepiju *ne, d<u>ee</u>-kee, ne-pee-yoo*
Dan nej tak, jeg drikker ikke *nai tahk, yai dre-kuhr ik-kuh*
Dut nee dank je, ik drink niet *nay dank ye, ik drink neet*
Fr non merci, je ne bois pas d'alcool *nON mair-see, zhuh nuh bwa pa dal-kol*
Ger nein danke, ich trinke nicht *neyn dang-kuh, ish tring-kuh nisht*
Gr όχι ευχαριστώ, δεν πίνω *o-hi ef-ha-ri-sto, then pi-no*
It no, grazie, non bevo *noh, grat-see-ay, non bay-voh*
Por não obrigado *(m)*/obrigada *(f)*, não bebo *noun oh-bree-gah-doo/ oh-bree-gah-dUH, noun bae-boo*
Sp gracias, no bebo *grath-yas, noh beb-oh*
Swe nej tack, jag dricker inte *ney tak, yahg dri-ker in-teh*

I'm drunk

Cz jsem opilej *(m)*/opilá *(f)* *ysem op-ee-ley/op-ee-l<u>a</u>*
Dan jeg er fuld *yai ehr fuhl*
Dut ik ben dronken *ik behn dronk-e(n)*
Fr je suis bourré *zhuh swee boo-ray*
Ger ich bin blau *ish bin blow*
Gr είμαι λιώμα *i-me li-o-ma*
It sono ubriaco *(m)*/ubriaca *(f)* *so-noh oob-ree-ah-koh/oob-ree-ah-ka*
Por estou bêbedo *(m)*/bêbeda *(f)* *esh-tow beh-bUH-doo/beh-bUH-dUH*
Sp estoy borracho *(m)*/borracha *(f)* *es-toy bo-RRa-choh/bo-RRa-cha*
Swe jag är full *yahg air full*

Fun fact!

You may think you're immersing yourself in the local culture with your pitcher of **Spanish sangria**, but in fact it's the quickest way to make yourself look like a tourist. Similar drinks more popular with young locals include **tinto de verano**, which is red wine with lemonade, or **calimocho** (spelled **kalimoxo** in the Basque region), red wine mixed with cola.

have you got a cigarette?

Cz	nemáš cigaretu?	*ne-m<u>a</u>sh **tsee**-gar-et-oo?*
Dan	har du en cigaret?	*haar doo ehn si-ga-**rett**?*
Dut	heb je misschien een sigaret?	*hehp je mis-**CHeen** en seeCH-ar-eht?*
Fr	est-ce que tu aurais une cigarette ?	*ess kuh tU or-ay Un see-ga-ret?*
Ger	hast du vielleicht eine Zigarette?	*hast doo vee-**leyCHt** ey-nuh tsi-ga-**ret**-uh?*
Gr	έχεις ένα τσιγάρο;	*e-his e-na tsi-**gha**-ro?*
It	hai una sigaretta?	*ah-ee oo-na see-gar-**ret**-ta?*
Por	tem um cigarro?	*taim oom see-**gah**-RRoo?*
Sp	¿tienes un cigarro?	*tyen-es oon thee-**gaRR**-oh?*
Swe	har du en cigarett?	*hahr doo en sig-a-**rett**?*

have you got a light?

Cz	nemáš oheň? *ne-mash o-heny?*
Dan	har du ild? *haar doo il?*
Dut	heb je misschien een vuurtje? *hehp je mis-CHeen en fuur-tye?*
Fr	est-ce que tu aurais du feu ? *ess kuh tU or-ay dU fuh?*
Ger	hast du mal Feuer? *hast doo mahl foy-uh?*
Gr	έχεις φωτιά; *e-his fo-ti-a?*
It	hai da accendere? *ah-ee da a-chen-der-ay?*
Por	tem lume? *taim loo-m?*
Sp	¿tienes fuego? *tyen-es fway-goh?*
Swe	har du eld? *hahr doo eld?*

do you mind if I smoke?

Cz	nevadí, když si zapálím? *ne-vad-ee, kdeezh see za-pal-eem?*
Dan	gør det noget, hvis jeg ryger? *goer deh no-wuht, vis yai rue-uhr?*
Dut	vind je het vervelend als ik rook? *find ye het fer-vayl-ent als ik rohk?*
Fr	ça te dérange si je fume ? *sa tuh day-rONzh see zhuh fUm?*
Ger	stört es dich wenn ich rauche? *steurt ess dish ven ish row-CHuh?*
Gr	σε πειράζει αν καπνίσω; *se pi-ra-zi an ka-pni-so?*
It	ti dà fastidio se fumo? *tee dah fa-stee-dee-oh say foo-moh?*
Por	importa-se que fume? *eem-pohr-tUH-sae kae foo-m?*
Sp	¿te importa que fume? *tay eem-por-ta kay foo-may?*
Swe	stör det dig om jag röker? *stur det day om yahg rur-ker?*

could you take a photo of us, please?

Cz	můžete nás fotit, prosím? *moozh-e-te nas fot-eet, pro-seem?*
Dan	vil du tage et billede af os? *vil doo tah ett bill-uh-THuh a oss?*
Dut	kunt u misschien een foto van ons maken? *kent oo mis-CHeen en foht-oh fan ons mahk-e(n)?*
Fr	est-ce que vous pourriez nous prendre en photo, s'il vous plaît ? *ess kuh voo poo-ree-ay noo prONdr ON foh-toh, seel voo play?*

98

Ger	könnten Sie bitte ein Foto von uns machen? *keun-tuhn zee bit-uh eyn foh-toh fon uns ma-CHuhn?*
Gr	μπορείτε να μας βγάλετε μία φωτογραφία, παρακαλώ; *bo-ri-te na mas vgha-le-te mi-a fo-togh-ra-fi-a, pa-ra-ka-lo?*
It	ci potrebbe fare una foto, per favore? *chee po-treb-bay fah-ray oo-na foh-toh, per fa-vor-ay?*
Por	importa-se de nos tirar uma fotografia, se faz favor? *eem-por-tUH-say dae noosh tee-rahr oo-mUH fo-too-grUH-fee-UH, s-fahsh fUH-vor?*
Sp	¿nos puede hacer una foto, por favor? *nos pway-day a-thair oo-na foh-toh, por fa-bor?*
Swe	kan du ta en bild på oss? *kan doo tah en bild paw oss?*

cheers!

Cz	na zdraví! *na zdra-vee!*
Dan	skål! *skawl!*
Dut	proost! *prohst!*
Fr	santé ! *sON-tay!*, tchin-tchin ! *cheen-cheen!*
Ger	prost! *prohst!*, zum Wohle! *tsum voh-luh!*
Gr	στην υγειά μας! *stin i-ya mas!*
It	cincin! *cheen-cheen!*
Por	saúde! *sUH-ood!*
Sp	¡salud! *sa-lood!*
Swe	skål! *skawl!*

Fun fact!

You should always look people in the eye when saying 'cheers' and clinking glasses: failure to do so is considered rude or unlucky in many cultures, and in **Germany** is said to bring you seven years' bad sex! Other European faux pas include putting your glass down without taking a sip first, and crossing your arm over someone else's when toasting.

♥ The Language of Love ♥

can I buy you a drink?

Cz můžu tě pozvat na skleničku?
*moozh-oo tye **poz**-vat **na** sklen-eech-koo?*

Dan vil du have noget at drikke?
*vil doo hah **no**-wuht att **dre**-kuh?*

Dut wil je iets drinken?
*vil ye eets **drink**-e(n)?*

Fr je t'offre un verre ?
zjuh tofr un vair?

Ger darf ich dir ein Getränk spendieren?
*darf ish deer eyn guh-**trenk** shpen-**deer**-uhn?*

Gr μπορώ να σε κεράσω ένα ποτό;
*bo-**ro** na se ke-**ra**-so **e**-na po-**to**?*

It posso offrirti qualcosa da bere?
*pos-soh of-**freer**-tee kwal-**koh**-za da **bay**-ray?*

Por posso pagar-lhe uma bebida?
*poh-soo pUH-**gahr**-lyee **oo**-mUH bae-**bee**-dUH?*

Sp ¿te puedo invitar a una copa?
*tay **pway**-doh een-bee-**tar** a **oo**-na **koh**-pa?*

Swe vill du ha något att dricka?
*vill doo hah **naw**-got att **dri**-ka?*

Club Classics

Vital vocab

club

Cz	klub	*kloob*
Dan	diskotek	*dis-koh-**tehk***
Dut	disco	***dis**-koh*
Fr	boîte	*bwat*
Ger	Club *kluhb*, Disko	***dis**-koh*
Gr	κλαμπ	*klab*
It	discoteca	*dees-koh-**tay**-ka*
Por	discoteca	*deesh-koo-**teh**-kUH*
Sp	discoteca	*dees-koh-**tay**-ka*
Swe	nattklubb	***nat**-kloob*

to go clubbing

Cz	chodit do klubů	*khod-eet **do** kloob-<u>oo</u>*
Dan	at gå på diskotek	*att gaw poe dis-koh-**tehk***
Dut	uitgaan	***euit**-CHahn*
Fr	aller en boîte	*al-ay on bwat*
Ger	auf Clubtour gehen *owf **kluhb**-toor **gay**-uhn*, ausgehen *ows-gay-uhn*
Gr	πάω στο κλαμπ	***pa**-o sto klab*
It	andare a ballare	*an-**dah**-ray a bal-**lah**-ray*
Por	ir à discoteca	*eer ah deesh-koo-**teh**-kUH*
Sp	ir a bailar	*eer a beye-lar*
Swe	gå på klubb	*gaw paw kloob*

In the Know

Clubbing is popular all over Europe and you should be able to find a venue to suit your taste: check local guides, pick up flyers in bars or from street promoters, or just ask around. If you're in a university town, it's worth checking out the student union or information centre if there is one. The minimum age for admission is usually 18 (often 21 in Sweden), though some places impose their own limits (such as 21 or 25) and may require ID.

Commercial dance music and European chart pop are played everywhere, while trance and techno are popular in many countries and there are generally a few places where you can sample authentic local music. Although strict dress codes are relatively rare, in most places people make a bit of an effort when going clubbing: avoid trainers, flip-flops, shorts and scruffy t-shirts if you're planning a big night out. The trendiest and most expensive clubs can have selective door policies. All the big cities have a decent gay scene, as do some of the popular Med resorts (in smaller towns it can be a bit limited): just ask around for the best places to go, or check out local what's on guides.

In Spain, Portugal, Greece and central and southern Italy, people tend to have long, late dinners and may not go out until 10 or 11 pm. Clubs don't get going until after midnight and are usually open until 5 or 6 am. French clubs have similar opening hours, and in France and the Mediterranean countries you can look for an **after** (a post-club party lasting into the morning) if you haven't had enough! In Spain, the real test is whether you can make it to a café for a breakfast of **churros y chocolate** (thick hot chocolate served with fritters for dunking). Clubs in these countries usually charge for admission (sometimes a reduced fee before midnight, or free for women), and this will often include a free drink. Live acts are very popular in Italian clubs, particularly in Rimini whose clubs are said to rival Ibiza's.

In Germany and the Czech Republic, clubs tend to shut around 2 or 3 (though some in big cities stay open till 5). Admission prices don't usually include a drink. Techno music is very popular in Germany and Holland, but if that's not your scene you could always look for a German club playing "oldies" (mainly 60s/70s music). Dutch clubs are sometimes free and drinks prices are similar to those in cafés and bars (though very trendy places usually charge more).

Drinks are expensive in Denmark and Sweden and even more so in clubs, so people often meet at someone's house for drinks before going out about 10 or 11 pm. They may go back to someone's house afterwards too (known in Sweden as an **efterfest** or after-party).

Over to you

are there any good hip-hop/house/salsa clubs around here?

Cz	jsou tady v okolí nějaké dobré hip-hopové/housové/salsa kluby? *yso-oo **tad**-ee v **ok**-ol-ee **nye**-yak-e **dob**-re heep-hop-ove/ ho-oos-ove/**sal**-sa **kloob**-ee?*
Dan	er der et godt diskotek i nærheden, hvor de spiller hip hop/ house/salsa? *ehr dehr eht gott dis-koh-**tehk** ee **nehr**-heTH-uhn, vor dee **spill**-uh hip hop/house/salsa?*
Dut	zijn er goede hip-hop/house/salsa clubs in de buurt? *zayn ehr **CHood**-e **hip**-hop/hows/**sal**-sa klebs in de buurt?*
Fr	est-ce qu'il y a des boîtes hip-hop/house/salsa sympas par ici ? *ess keel ya day bwat eep-op/ows/sal-sa sAN-pa par ee-see?*
Ger	gibt's hier in der Nähe irgendwelche guten Hiphopclubs/ Houseclubs/Salsaclubs? *geepts heer in dehr **neh**-uh **eer**-guhnd-vel-shuh **goo**-tuhn **hip**-hop-kluhbs/**hows**-kluhbs/**sal**-sa-kluhbs?*
Gr	υπάρχει κανένα κλαμπ με χιπ-χοπ/χάουζ/σάλσα μουσική εδώ γύρω; *i-**par**-hi ka-**ne**-na klab me **hip**-hop/**ha**-ooz/**sal**-sa moo-si-**ki** e-**tho** ghi-ro?*

It   ci sono dei bei locali di hip hop/house/ latino-americano da queste parti? *chee **so**-noh **day**-ee **bay**-ee lo-**kah**-lee dee eep op/ows/la-**tee**-noh-a-may-ree-**kah**-noh da **kwes**-tay **par**-tee?*

Por   há alguma discoteca boa aqui perto que passe hip-hop/house music/salsa? *ah al-goo-mUH deesh-koo-**teh**-kUH bo-UH UH-**kee** pehr-too kae pass **hip**-hop/house moo-zeek/**sal**-sa?*

Sp   ¿hay alguna buena discoteca de hip-hop/house/salsa por aquí? *eye al-**goo**-na **bway**-na dees-koh-**tay**-ka day **heep**-hop/house/**sal**-sa por a-**kee**?*

Swe   finns det någon bra hip-hop/house/salsa klubb här? *finns det **naw**-gon brah **hip**-hop/hows/**sal**-sa kloob hair?*

I prefer rock/R & B/drum and bass

Cz   radši mám rock/R & B/drum and bass *rad-shee m**a**m rok/**ar**-n-bee/droom end bas*

Dan   jeg kan bedst lide rock/R & B/drum og bass *yai kan best lee rok/ar-n-**bee**/drum oe bays*

Dut   ik houd het meest van rock/R & B/drum and bass *ik how het mayst van rok/ehr en bay/drem en bays*

Fr   je préfère le rock/le R & B/le drum'n'bass *zhuh pray-fair luh rok/le ar-n-bee/le drum-n-bays*

Ger   ich mag am liebsten Rock/R & B/Drum'n'Bass *ish mahg am **leep**-stuhn rok/ar-n-**bee**/drum-n-**bays***

Gr   προτιμώ ροκ μουσική/ριθμ εντ μπλουζ/ντραμ εντ μπας *pro-ti-mo rok moo-si-**ki**/ri-THm ed blooz/dram end bas*

It   preferisco il rock/il rhythm'n'blues/il drum and bass *pray-fay-**rees**-koh eel rock/eel **reet**-am an blooz/eel dram an bays*

Por   prefiro rock/R & B/drum and bass *prae-**fee**-roo rok/ahr-n-**bee**/drum-n-**bays***

Sp   prefiero el rock/el R & B/el drum and bass *pray-**fyair**-oh el rok/el ar-en-**bee**/el drum en bays*

Swe   jag föredrar rock/R & B/drum och bass *yahg **fur**-eh-drar rok/ar-n-**bee**/drum och bahs*

what sort of music do they play?

Cz	jaký druh muziky hrajou? *yak-<u>ee</u> drookh mooz-ee-kee hra-yo-oo?*
Dan	hvilken slags musik spiller de? *vil-kuhn slahks mu-**seek** **spill**-uh dee?*
Dut	watvoor soort muziek spelen ze? *vat for sohrt moo-**ziek** spayl-e(n) ze?*
Fr	ils passent quel genre de musique ? *eel pass kel zhONr duh mU-zeek?*
Ger	was für Musik wird da gespielt? *vas <u>fuur</u> moo-**zeek** veerd dah guh-**shpeelt**?*
Gr	τι μουσική παίζουν; *ti moo-si-ki **pe**-zoon?*
It	che tipo di musica c'è? *kay **tee**-poh dee moo-**zee**-ka chay?*
Por	que género de música tocam? *kae **zhehn**-roo dae moo-zee-k**UH** toh-kou**ŋ**?*
Sp	¿qué tipo de música ponen? *kay **tee**-poh day moo-see-ka **poh**-nen?*
Swe	vilken sorts musik spelar de? *vil-ken sorts moo-**seek** **speel**-ar dom?*

Fun fact!

Famous clubs in unusual locations include **Prague**'s five-storey **Karlovy lázně** club, housed in a 15th century former spa building, **Amsterdam**'s **Paradiso**, a rock club in an old church, and **Paris**'s **Batofar**, on a barge moored on the Seine.

what time does it open/close?

Cz	v kolik hodin otvírají/zavírají?	*v **kol**-eek **hod**-een **ot**-veer-ay-<u>ee</u>/za-veer-ay-<u>ee</u>?*
Dan	hvornår åbner/lukker det?	*vor-**naw** awb-nuh/**luh**-kuh deh?*
Dut	hoe laat gaat het open/dicht?	*hoo laht CHaht het **ohp**-e(n)/diCHt?*
Fr	ça ouvre/ferme à quelle heure ?	*sa oovr/fairm a kel uhr?*
Ger	wann machen die auf/zu?	*van **ma**-CHun dee owf/tsoo?*
Gr	τι ώρα ανοίγει/κλείνει;	*ti **o**-ra a-**ni**-ghi/**kli**-ni?*
It	a che ora apre/chiude?	*a kay **o**-ra **ap**-ray/**kyoo**-day?*
Por	a que horas abre/fecha?	*UH kae oh-rUHsh **ah**-brae/**fae**-shUH?*
Sp	¿a qué hora abre/cierra?	*a kay **or**-a **ab**-ray/**thyai**RR-a?*
Swe	när öppnar/stänger de?	*nair **up**-nar/**steng**-ar dom?*

how much is it to get in?

Cz	kolik stojí vstupné?	***kol**-eek **stoy**-ee vs-**toop**-ne?*
Dan	hvad koster det at komme ind?	*vaTH **kos**-tuhr deh att **kom**-muh inn?*
Dut	hoeveel is de entree?	*hoo-**vayl** is de ahn-**tray**?*
Fr	combien coûte l'entrée ?	*kON-byAN koot l'ON-tray?*
Ger	was kostet der Eintritt?	*vas **kos**-tuht dehr **eyn**-trit?*
Gr	πόσο κοστίζει η είσοδος;	***po**-so kos-**ti**-zi i **i**-so-thos?*
It	quanto costa l'ingresso?	***kwan**-toh **kos**-ta leen-**gres**-soh?*
Por	quanto custa a entrada?	*kwUHn-too koosh-tUH UH ain-**trah**-dUH?*
Sp	¿cuánto es la entrada?	***kwan**-toh es la en-**trah**-da?*
Swe	hur mycket kostar inträdet?	*hoor **muk**-eh **kos**-tar in-**traid**-et?*

is there a dress code?

Cz	mám si vzít nějaké speciální oblečení?	*m<u>a</u>m see vzeet **nye**-yak-<u>e</u> **spets**-ee-<u>al</u>-nee **ob**-lech-en-<u>ee</u>?*
Dan	er der en bestemt dress code?	*ehr dehr eyn beh-**stemt** dress kohd?*

Dut	is er een dress code? *is ehr en drehs kohd?*
Fr	est-ce qu'il y a un dress code ? *ess keel ya AN dress kohd?*
Ger	gibt's da einen Dresscode? *geepts dah **eyn**-uhn dress-kohd?*
Gr	πώς πρέπει να ντυθούμε; *pos **pre**-pi na di-**THoo**-me?*
It	bisogna vestirsi eleganti? *bee-**zon**-ya ves-**teer**-see ay-lay-**gan**-tee?*
Por	existe algum código de vestuário? *ee-**zeesh**-t al-**goom** koh-dee-goo dae vesh-**twah**-ree-oo?*
Sp	¿cómo hay que ir vestido? *ko-moh eye kay eer bes-**tee**-doh?*
Swe	finns det någon dresskod? *finns det **naw**-gon dress-kood?*

where's the cloakroom?

Cz	kde je (tu) šatna? *kde ye (too) **shat**-na?*
Dan	hvor er garderoben? *vor ehr gahr-duh-**roh**-buhn?*
Dut	waar is de garderobe? *vahr is de CHard-e-**roh**-be?*
Fr	où est le vestiaire ? *oo ay luh ves-**tyair**?*
Ger	wo ist die Garderobe? *voh ist dee gar-duh-**roh**-buh?*
Gr	πού είναι η γκαρνταρόμπα; *poo **i**-ne i gar-da-**ro**-ba?*
It	dov'è il guardaroba? *doh-**vay** eel gwar-da-**roh**-ba?*
Por	onde é o vestiário? *ond eh oo vesh-tee-**ah**-ree-oo?*
Sp	¿dónde está el ropero? *don-day es-ta el roh-**pair**-oh?*
Swe	var ligger garderoben? *var **ligg**-er gard-**roob**-en?*

are there any gay clubs?

Cz	jsou tady nějaké gay kluby? *yso-oo **tad**-ee **nye**-yak-e̠ gey **kloob**-ee?*
Dan	er der et diskotek for homoseksuelle? *ehr dehr eht dis-koh-**tehk** for **hoh**-moh-sex-u-ell-uh?*
Dut	zijn er gay clubs? *zayn er gay klebs?*
Fr	est-ce qu'il y a des boîtes gay ? *ess keel ya day bwat gay?*
Ger	gibt's auch Clubs für Schwule und Lesben? *geepts owCH kluhbs fuur **shvoo**-luh und **lez**-buhn?*
Gr	υπάρχουν κλαμπς για γκέι; *i-**par**-hoon klabs ya **ge**-i?*
It	ci sono delle discoteche gay? *chee **so**-noh **del**-lay dees-koh-**tay**-kay gay?*

Club Classics (side tab)

Por	há alguma discoteca gay? *ah al-**goo**-ma deesh-koo-**teh**-kUH gay?*
Sp	¿hay discotecas de ambiente? *eye dees-koh-**tay**-kas day am-**byen**-tay?*
Swe	finns det någon gayklubb? *finns det **naw**-gon **gay**-kloob?*

Fun fact!

Amsterdam was until recently known as the gay capital of Europe. The crown has now been taken by London (though several other cities make the same claim!), but Amsterdam still has a thriving gay scene and plenty of clubs to choose from.

the DJ's really cool/lousy

Cz	ten dýdžej je fakt skvělej/lůzr *ten **dee**-dzhey ye fakt **skvyel**-ey/<u>loo</u>zr*
Dan	DJ'en er ret god/dårlig ***dee**-jay-uhn ehr rett goh/**dawr**-lee*
Dut	de DJ is erg goed/slecht *de **dee**-jay is ehrCH CHoot/sleCHt*
Fr	le DJ est vraiment cool/nul *luh dee-jay ay vray-mON kool/nUl*
Ger	der DJ ist echt klasse/mies *dehr **dee**-jay ist eCHt **klas**-uh/mees*
Gr	ο ντι-τζέι είναι πολύ κουλ/χάλια *o **di**-tze-i **i**-ne po-**li** kool/**ha**-li-a*
It	il DJ è fortissimo/fa pena *eel **dee**-jay ay for-**tees**-see-moh/fah **pay**-na*
Por	o DJ é muito bom/é péssimo *oo **dee**-jay eh **mooy**-too bom/eh **peh**-see-moo*
Sp	el DJ es muy bueno/es malísimo *el dee-**jay** es mwee **bway**-noh/es mal-**ees**-ee-moh*

109

Swe DJ'n är verkligen jättebra/botten *dee-jay-en air **verk**-lig-en ye-teh-**bra**/**bott**-en*

this place is cool/a bit cheesy!

Cz tohle místo je skvělý/trochu díra! *toh-le **meest**-o ye **skvyel**-<u>ee</u>/**trokh**-oo <u>deer</u>-a!*

Dan her er ret fedt/lidt dårligt! *hehr ehr rett fett/lit **dawr**-lit!*

Dut dit is een leuke/saaie [club/café/etc]! *dit is en **leuk**-e/**seye**-e [kleb/ka-**fay**]!*

Fr c'est cool/un peu ringard ici ! *say kool/AN puh rAN-gar ee-see!*

Ger es ist hier wirklich cool/ein bisschen schmierig! *ess ist heer **veerk**-liCH kool/eyn **bis**-shuhn **shmeer**-ig!*

Gr αυτό το μέρος είναι ωραίο/λίγο βαρετό! *af-**to** to **me**-ros **i**-ne o-**re**-o/**li**-gho va-re-**to**!*

It questo posto è una figata/un po' kitsch! *kwes-toh **pos**-toh ay **oo**-na fee-**gah**-ta/oon po keetsh!*

Por este local é porreiro/um pouco rasca! *aesht loo-**kahl** eh poo-**RRay**-roo/oom **po**-koo **RRahsh**-kUH!*

Sp ¡este sitio es guay/un poco hortera! *es-tay **see**-tyoh es gweye/oon **poh**-koh or-**tair**-a!*

Swe det här stället är fantastiskt/rätt uselt! *det hair **stel**-et air fan-**tast**-iskt/rett **oos**-elt!*

there are some really sleazy guys in here

Cz jsou tady nějaký fakt nechutný lidi *yso-oo **tad**-ee **ney**-yak-<u>ee</u> fakt ne-khoot-n<u>ee</u> **leed**-ee*

Dan der er nogle ret klamme fyrer her *dehr ehr **no**-nuh rett **klah**-muh **fuer**-uh hehr*

Dut er zijn een aantal hele foute mannen hier *ehr zayn en **ahn**-tal **hayl**-e **fowt**-e **man**-e(n) heer*

Fr il y a des mecs vraiment louches ici *eel ya day mek vray-mON loosh ee-see*

Ger hier laufen voll die schmierigen Typen rum *heer **low**-fuhn fol dee **shmeer**-ig-uhn **tee**-puhn rum*

110

Gr	υπάρχουν μερικοί πολύ περίεργοι τύποι εδώ μέσα *i-par-hoon me-ri-ki po-li pe-ri-er-ghi ti-pi e-tho me-sa*
It	ci sono dei tipi poco raccomandabili qui *chee so-noh day-ee tee-pee poh-koh rak-kom-man-dah-bee-lee kwee*
Por	alguns tipos aqui são asquerosos *al-goonsh tee-poosh UH-kee soun UHhsh-kae-roh-zoosh*
Sp	hay una gente super chunga ahí dentro *eye oo-na CHen-tay soo-pair choong-ga a-ee den-troh*
Swe	det finns vissa verkligt sjaskiga typer här *det finns viss-a verkligt shask-ig-a toop-er hair*

would you like to dance?

Cz	nechceš si zatancovat? *nekh-tsesh see za-tants-ov-at?*
Dan	vil du danse? *vil doo dan-suh?*
Dut	wil je dansen? *vil ye dans-e(n)?*
Fr	tu veux danser ? *tU vuh dON-say?*
Ger	hast du Lust mit mir zu tanzen? *hast doo lust mit meer tsoo tan-tsuhn?*
Gr	θέλεις να χορέψεις; *THe-lis na ho-rep-sis?*
It	vuoi ballare? *voo-oh-ee bal-lah-ray?*
Por	quer dançar? *kehr dUHn-sahr?*
Sp	¿quieres bailar? *kyair-es beye-lar?*
Swe	vill du dansa? *vil doo dans-a?*

you're very beautiful

Cz	jsi moc hezká *ysee mots hez-ka*
Dan	du er meget smuk *doo ehr mai-yuht smoek*
Dut	je bent erg mooi *ye behnt ehrCH moo-ee*
Fr	tu es vraiment jolie *tU ay vray-mON jo-lee*
Ger	du bist wirklich umwerfend *doo bist veerk-liCH um-vehr-fuhnd*
Gr	είσαι πολύ όμορφη *i-se po-li o-mor-fi*
It	sei molto bella *say-ee mol-toh bel-la*
Por	é muito bonita *eh mooy-too boo-nee-tUH*

Sp	eres muy guapa *e-res mwee **gwa**-pa*
Swe	du är mycket vacker *doo air **muk**-eh **vak**-er*

he's/she's gorgeous!

Cz	on je úžasnej (m)/ona je úžasná (f)! *on ye **oozh**-asn-ey/**on**-a ye oozh-asn-__a__!*
Dan	han/hun er lækker! *han/huen ehr **leh**-kuh!*
Dut	hij/zij is erg knap! *hay/zay is ehrCH knap!*
Fr	il/elle est canon ! *eel/el ay ca-nON!*
Ger	der/die ist der absolute Hammer! *dehr/dee ist dehr ab-so-**loo**-tuh **ham**-uh!*
Gr	είναι κούκλος (m)/κούκλα (f) *i-ne **koo**-klos/**koo**-kla!*
It	è carino (m)/carina (f) da morire! *ay ka-**ree**-noh/ka-**ree**-na da mo-**ree**-ray!*
Por	ele é muito giro (m)/ela é muito gira (f)! *ehl eh **mooy**-too zhee-roo/ehl-UH eh **mooy**-too zhee-rUH!*
Sp	¡está buenísimo (m)/buenísima (f)! *es-**ta** bway-**nees**-ee-moh/bway-**nees**-ee-ma!*
Swe	han/hon är dösnygg! *han/hoon air **dur**-snug!*

thanks, but I'm with my boyfriend/girlfriend

Cz	díky, ale jsem tady s přítelem/s přítelkyní *__deek__-ee, al-e ysem tad-ee s przh__eet__-el-em/s przh__eet__-el-keen-__ee__*
Dan	tak, men jeg er her med min kæreste *tahk, mehn yai ehr hehr meTH meen **kehr**-stuh*
Dut	dank je, maar ik ben hier met mijn vriend/vriendin *dank ye, mahr ik behn heer meht mayn freend/**freend**-in*
Fr	merci, mais je suis avec mon copain/ma copine *mair-see, may zhuh sweez a-vek mon ko-pAN/ma ko-peen*
Ger	danke, aber ich bin mit meinem Freund/meiner Freundin hier *__dang__-kuh, __ah__-buh ish bin mit **mey**-nuhm froynd/**mey**-nuh **froynd**-in heer*
Gr	ευχαριστώ, αλλά είμαι με τον φίλο/φίλη μου *ef-ha-ri-**sto**,a-la i-me me ton **fi**-lo/**fi**-li moo*

Club Classics

It	grazie, ma sono con il mio ragazzo/la mia ragazza *grat-see-ay, ma so-noh kon eel mee-oh ra-gat-soh/la mee-a ra-gat-sa*
Por	obrigado *(m)*/obrigada *(f)*, mas estou com o meu namorado/a minha namorada *oh-bree-gah-doo/oh-bree-gah-dUH, mUHsh esh-tow kom oo may-oo nUH-moo-rah-doo/UH meen-yUH nUH-moo-rah-dUH*
Sp	gracias, pero estoy con mi novio/novia *grath-yas, pe-roh es-toy kon mee noh-byoh/noh-bya*
Swe	tack, men jag är här med min kille/tjej *tak, men yahg air hair med min kill-eh/shay*

> **Fun fact!**
>
> Clubbing in the north of **Sweden** in summer can be a surreal experience, as the midnight sun means your whole night out takes place in broad daylight!

Club Classics

Listen up!

would you like to come clubbing with us later?

Cz	nechceš s námi potom jít někam do klubu? *nekh-tsesh s nam-ee pot-om yeet nyek-am do kloob-oo?*
Dan	vil du med i byen med os senere? *vil doo meTH ee bue-uhn meTH oss sehn-uhr?*
Dut	heb je zin om met ons mee uit te gaan later? *hehp ye zin om meht ons may euit te CHahn lah-ter?*

Fr	est-ce que tu veux venir en boîte avec nous plus tard ? *ess kuh tU vuh vuh-neer ON bwat a-vek noo plU tar?*
Ger	hast du Lust nachher mit uns herumzuziehen? *hast doo lust naCH-hehr mit uns hehr-rum-tsoo-tsee-uhn?*
Gr	θάθελες να έρθεις σ'ένα κλαμπ μαζί μας αργότερα; *THa-THe-les na er-THis se-na klab ma-zi mas ar-gho-te-ra?*
It	ti va di andare a ballare con noi più tardi? *tee va dee an-dah-ray a bal-lah-ray kon noh-ee pyoo tar-dee?*
Por	quer ir connosco à discoteca mais tarde? *kehr eer kon-nosh-koo ah deesh-koo-teh-kUH mah-eesh tahrd?*
Sp	¿quieres venir a bailar con nosotros luego? *kyair-es ben-eer a beye-lar kon nos-ot-ros lway-goh?*
Swe	vill du gå på klubb med oss senare? *vill doo gaw paw kloob med oss sen-ahr-eh?*

the admission fee includes a free drink

Cz	v ceně vstupného je jedno pití zdarma *v tsen-ye vstoop-ne-ho ye yed-no peet-ee zdar-ma*
Dan	der er en gratis drink med i entréen *dehr ehr ehn graa-tees drehnk meTH ee en-tray-uhn*
Dut	je krijgt een gratis drankje voor de entree *ye krayCHt en CHrat-is drank-ye voor de ahn-tray*
Fr	l'entrée donne droit à une boisson gratuite *lON-tray don drwa a Un bwa-sON gra-tweet*
Ger	mit der Eintrittskarte kriegt man ein kostenloses Getränk *mit dehr eyn-trits-kahr-tuh kreekt man eyn kos-tuhn-loh-zuhs guh-trenk*
Gr	η είσοδος συμπεριλαμβάνει κι ένα ποτό δωρεάν *i i-so-thos si-be-ri-lam-va-ni ki-e-na po-to tho-re-an*
It	c'è una consumazione compresa nel biglietto *chay oo-na kon-soo-mat-see-oh-nay kom-pray-za nel bee-lyet-toh*
Por	a entrada inclui uma bebida grátis *UH ain-trah-dUH een-klooy oo-mUH bae-bee-dUH grah-teesh*
Sp	la entrada incluye una consumición *la en-trah-da een-kloo-yay oo-na kon-soo-meeth-yohn*

114

Swe det ingår en gratis drink i inträdet *det in-gaw en gra-tis drink i in-traid-et*

can I see some ID, please?

Cz můžu vidět nějaký průkaz, prosím? *m<u>oo</u>zh-oo veed-yet nye-yak-ee pr<u>oo</u>-kaz, pro-seem?*

Dan må jeg se noget ID, tak? *maw yai sey no-wuht ee-dey, tahk?*

Dut kun je je paspoort laten zien, alsjeblieft? *ken ye ye pas-port lah-ten zeen, als-ye-bleeft?*

Fr est-ce que vous avez une pièce d'identité, s'il vous plaît ? *ess kuh vooz a-vay Un pyess dee-dON-tee-tay, seel voo play?*

Ger den Ausweis bitte *dayn ows-veys bit-uh*

Gr μπορώ να δω την ταυτότητά σας, παρακαλώ; *bo-ro na tho tin taf-to-ti-ta sas, pa-ra-ka-lo?*

It posso vedere un documento di identità, per favore? *pos-soh vay-day-ray oon do-koo-men-toh dee ee-den-tee-tah, per fa-vor-ay?*

Por posso ver o BI, se faz favor? *poh-soo vehr oo bay-ee, s-fahsh fUH-vor?*

Sp ¿carnet de identidad, por favor? *kar-net day ee-den-tee-dad, por fa-bor?*

Swe kan jag få se er legitimation? *kan yahg faw see er leg-it-i-ma-shoon?*

you can't come in with trainers/a football shirt on

Cz v teniskách/ve fotbalovém dresu dovnitř nemůžete *v ten-ees-k<u>a</u>kh/ve fot-bal-ov-<u>e</u>m dresu dov-neetzhr ne-m<u>oo</u>zh-ete*

Dan du kan ikke komme ind med kondisko/en fodboldtrøje *doo kan ik-kuh kom-muh in meTH kon-dee-skoe/ehn foeTH-bohld-troe-yuh*

Dut je mag niet binnen met gympen/een voetbalshirt aan *ye maCH neet bin-ne(n) meht gim-pe(n)/en foot-bal-shert ahn*

Fr vous ne pouvez pas rentrer en baskets/avec un maillot de foot *voo nuh poo-vay pa rON-tray ON bas-ket/a-vek AN meye-oh duh foot*

115

Ger	hier kommst du mit Sportklamotten/Fußballtrikots nicht rein
	*heer komst doo mit **shport**-kla-mot-uhn/**fus**-bal-tri-kohs nisht reyn*
Gr	δεν μπορείτε να μπείτε με αθλητικά παπούτσια/με αθλητική
	μπλούζα *then bo-**ri**-te na **bi**-te me a-THli-ti-**ka** pa-**poo**-tsi-a/me*
	*a-THli-ti-**ki bloo**-za*
It	non si può entrare in scarpe da ginnastica/maglietta da calcio
	*non see pwo en-**trah**-ray een **skar**-pay da jeen-**nas**-tee-ka/ma-**lyet**-ta da **kal**-choh*
Por	não pode entrar de sapatilhas/com uma camisola de futebol
	*noun pod ain-**trahr** dae sUH-pUH-**teel**-yUHsh/kom **oo**-mUH kUH-mee-**zoh**-lUH dae foot-**bol***
Sp	no puedes entrar en zapatillas/con camiseta de fútbol *noh **pway**-des en-**trar** en tha-pa-**tee**-yas/kon ka-mee-**set**-a day **foot**-bol*
Swe	ni får inte komma in med gympadojor/fotbollströja *nee faw in-teh **kom**-a in med yum-pa-**doo**-yor/foot-bolls-**trur**-ya*

your place or mine?

Cz půjdem k tobě nebo ke mně?
***poo**-ydem k **tob**-ye nebo **ke** mnye?*

Dan dit eller mit sted?
*deet el-**luh** meet steTH?*

Dut bij jou of bij mij?
bay yow of bay may?

Fr chez toi ou chez moi ?
shay twa oo shay mwa?

Ger zu dir oder zu mir?
*tsoo deer **oh**-duh tsoo meer?*

Gr σπίτι σου ή σπίτι μου;
***spi**-ti soo i **spi**-ti moo?*

116

It facciamo da me o da te?
fa-chah-moh da may oh da tay?

Por na sua casa ou na minha?
nUH soo-UH kah-zUH o nUH meen-yUH?

Sp ¿mi casa o la tuya?
mee ka-sa oh la too-ya?

Swe ditt eller mitt ställe?
dit ell-er mit stel-eh?

Culture Vultures

Vital vocab

film

Cz	film	*feelm*
Dan	film	*film*
Dut	film	*film*
Fr	film	*feelm*
Ger	Film	*film*
Gr	φιλμ *film*, έργο **er**-*gho*	
It	film	*feelm*
Por	filme	***feel**-m*
Sp	película	*pel-**ee**-koo-la*
Swe	film	*film*

cinema

Cz	kino	**kee**-*no*
Dan	biograf	*bee-o-**graaf***
Dut	bioscoop	*bee-o-**skohp***
Fr	cinéma	*see-**nay**-ma*
Ger	Kino	**kee**-*noh*
Gr	κινηματογράφος *ki-ni-ma-to-**ghra**-fos*, σινεμά *si-ne-**ma***	
It	cinema	**chee**-*nay-ma*
Por	cinema	*see-**nay**-mUH*
Sp	cine	*thee-**nay***
Swe	bio	**bee**-*o*

theatre

Cz	divadlo	*deev-ad-lo*
Dan	teater	*teh-ah-tuhr*
Dut	theater	*tay-ah-ter*
Fr	théâtre	*tay-ahtr*
Ger	Theater	*tay-ah-tuh*
Gr	θέατρο	*THe-a-tro*
It	teatro	*tay-at-roh*
Por	teatro	*tee-ah-troo*
Sp	teatro	*tay-ah-troh*
Swe	teater	*tee-ar-ter*

play

Cz	hra	*hra*
Dan	teaterstykke	*teh-ah-tuhr-stue-kuh*
Dut	toneelstuk	*toh-nayl-stek*
Fr	pièce	*pyess*
Ger	Theaterstück	*tay-ah-tuh-shtuuk*
Gr	παράσταση	*pa-ra-sta-si*
It	commedia	*kom-may-dee-a*
Por	peça de teatro	*peh-sUH dae tee-ah-troo*
Sp	obra de teatro	*ob-ra day tay-ah-troh*
Swe	pjäs	*pee-ais*

dance

Cz	tanec	*tan-ets*
Dan	dans	*danss*
Dut	dans	*dans*
Fr	danse	*dahns*
Ger	Tanz	*tants*
Gr	χορός	*ho-ros*
It	danza	*dant-sa*
Por	dança	*dan-sUH*
Sp	danza	*dan-tha*
Swe	dans	*dans*

Culture Vultures

119

show

Cz	představení	*przhed-stav-en-ee*
Dan	forestilling	*for-ruh-stil-ling*
Dut	voorstelling	*for-stel-ing*
Fr	spectacle	*spek-takl*
Ger	Auftritt *owf-trit*, Show *shoh*	
Gr	θέαμα	*THe-a-ma*
It	spettacolo	*spet-ta-koh-loh*
Por	espectáculo	*esh-peh-tah-koo-loo*
Sp	actuación	*ak-too-a-thyohn*
Swe	show	*show*

In the Know

To find out what's going on locally, you can either pick up a guide (eg **Guia del Ocio** in Spanish cities, **Přehled kulturních pořadů** in Prague, **Pariscope** in Paris) or check the Internet (Portuguese cities have an online **agenda cultural**; Copenhagen has a website called **www.aok.dk** with English content).

Going to the cinema is a popular pastime all over Europe. In France, Spain, Germany and Italy, English-language films are usually dubbed, although arts cinemas will often show films in the original language. In Scandinavia, Portugal, Greece, the Netherlands and the Czech Republic, English-language films are subtitled instead (though children's films are dubbed). Often, Czech cinemas even show Czech films with English subtitles. Cinemas in the warmer countries tend to have slightly later opening hours than those in the UK. In summer, many French towns organize outdoor film screenings. Many European cities hold their own film festivals (Cannes, Venice and the Berlinale are some of the best known, but there are plenty of more low-key events): check the local press and guides for details.

Going to the theatre tends to be a more formal affair and people dress fairly smartly. Plays are generally performed in the local language. If you're in Athens, try and catch a performance in the ancient open-air theatre of **Hρώδιο** (*i-ro-thi-o*): there are plenty of dance events, or you could brave a Greek play! Theatre buffs should also look out for the Epidaurus Festival in the Peloponnese, which runs through the summer months and is a chance to experience classical Greek drama in an ancient open-air theatre (synopses in English are available). France's **Festival d'Avignon** in July is another major theatre festival, with dozens of official performances plus a large fringe scene (**le off**). Italy is known as the home of opera and it's still very popular there – Verona's open-air performances in particular draw large crowds.

Most cities run a varied cultural programme throughout the year. In Copenhagen, look out for the annual **Kulturnatten** (culture night), usually held in October: tourist attractions are open until late at night, with cultural events and exhibitions organized all over the city. A special pass gives you access to all of them. Amsterdam has a similar event called **Museumnacht** (museum night), where all the museums stay open till 2 am and host DJs and other performances. Look out also for the **Uitmarkt** at the end of August, a weekend of shows, concerts and events marking the start of the new cultural season.

Traditional festivals are always a good way to join in with the locals and get a taste of the culture. In Spain and southern France, every town and village has its own summer festival with food, music and dancing. The Catholic countries avidly celebrate saints' days and religious festivals (Easter week is particularly important in Spain), and many regions have seasonal events linked to food and drink. In Portugal, there are major celebrations for student 'rag week': the most impressive take place in Coimbra in May and are known as the **Queima das Fitas** ('Burning of the Ribbons'). In Denmark and particularly Sweden, Midsummer is the biggest event of the year after Christmas.

Most cultural events offer discounts for students, and sometimes anyone under 26. Students should get an International Student Identity Card (ISIC) which will be recognized everywhere.

Over to you

is there a guide to what's on?

Cz je nějaký kulturní přehled? *ye nye-yak-ee kool-toor-nee przhe-hled?*

Dan er der en guide med hvad der sker? *ehr der ehn gaid meTH va der skehr?*

Dut is er een uitkrant? *is ehr en euit-krant?*

Fr est-ce qu'il y a un guide des spectacles ? *ess keel ya AN geed day spek-takl?*

Ger gibt es einen Veranstaltungskalender? *geept ess ey-nuhn fehr-an-shtalt-tungs-ka-len-duh?*

Gr υπάρχει κάποιος οδηγός θεαμάτων; *i-pa-rhi ka-pi-os o-thi-ghos THe-a-ma-ton?*

It c'è un programma degli spettacoli? *chay oon pro-gram-ma de-lyee spet-ta-koh-lee?*

Por há algum guia de espectáculos? *ah al-goom gee-ya desh-peh-tah-koo-loosh?*

Sp ¿hay una guía del ocio? *eye oo-na gee-a del ohth-yoh?*

Swe finns det någon nöjesguide? *finns det naw-gon noys-guide?*

what time does it start?

Cz kdy to začíná? *kdee to za-chee-na?*

Dan hvornår begynder det? *vor-nawr be-gue-nuhr deh?*

Dut hoe laat begint het? *hoo laht be-CHint het?*

Fr ça commence à quelle heure ? *sa ko-mONs a kel uhr?*

Ger wann fängt es an? *van fenkt ess an?*

Gr τι ώρα αρχίζει; *ti o-ra ar-hi-zi?*

It a che ora comincia? *a kay or-a kom-een-cha?*

Por a que horas começa? *UH kae oh-rUHsh koo-meh-sUH?*

Sp ¿a qué hora empieza? *a kay or-a em-pyay-tha?*

Swe vilken tid börjar det? *vil-ken teed bur-yar det?*

Fun fact!

For an unusual venue, visit **Prague**: on the last weekend in May the **Bohnice** psychiatric hospital opens its doors to the public for the **Mezi ploty** (Between the Fences) theatre and music festival!

I'd like [number] tickets for ...

Cz chtěl (m)/chtěla (f) bych [...] vstupenky na ... *khtyel/khtyel-a beekh [...] vstoo-pen-kee na ...*

Dan jeg vil gerne have [...] billetter til ... *yai vil gern hah [...] bee-lett-uhr till ...*

Dut ik wil graag [...] kaartjes voor... *ik vil CHrahCH [...] kahrt-yes for ...*

Fr je voudrais [...] places pour ... *zhuh voo-dray [...] plass poor ...*

Ger ich möchte [...] Karten für ... *ish meush-tuh [...] kahr-tuhn fuur ...*

Gr θα ήθελα [...] εισιτήρια για ... *THα i-THe-la [...] i-si-ti-ri-a ya ...*

It vorrei [...] biglietti per... *vor-ray-ee [...] bee-lyet-tee per...*

Por queria [...] bilhetes para ... *ke-ree-ya [...] beel-yae-tesh pUH-rUH ...*

Sp quería [...] entradas para ... *kair-ee-ya [...] en-trah-das pa-ra ...*

Swe jag skulle vilja ha [...] platser till ... *yahg skool-eh vil-ya hah [...] plat-ser till ...*

do we need to book in advance?

Cz	je třeba rezervovat předem? *ye **trzhe**-ba **rez**-er-vo-vat **przhe**-dem?*

Dan skal man bestille plads i forvejen? *skall man be-**still**-uh plass ee **for**-vai-uhn?*

Dut moet je van tevoren reserveren? *moot ye van te-**vor**-e(n) re-ser-**vayr**-e(n)?*

Fr est-ce qu'il faut réserver à l'avance ? *ess keel foh ray-zer-vay a la-vONs?*

Ger muss man die Karten vorbestellen? *mus man dee **kahr**-tuhn **for**-buh-shtel-uhn?*

Gr πρέπει να κρατήσουμε θέσεις από πριν; *pre-pi na kra-**ti**-soo-me THe-sis a-po prin?*

It dobbiamo prenotare in anticipo? *dob-bee-**ah**-moh pray-noh-**tah**-ray een an-**tee**-chee-poh?*

Por é preciso reservar antes? *eh prae-**see**-zoo RRae-zer-**vahr** UHn-tesh?*

Sp ¿hay que reservar con antelación? *eye kay res-air-**bar** kon an-tay-lath-**yohn**?*

Swe måste man boka i förväg? *mos-teh man **book**-a i fur-**vaig**?*

how much are the tickets?

Cz kolik stojí lístky? *kol-eek **stoy**-ee **leest**-kee?*

Dan hvad koster billetterne? *vaTH **koss**-tuhr bee-**lett**-uhr-nuh?*

Dut hoeveel kosten de kaartjes? *hoo-**vayl** kost-e(n) de **kahrt**-jes?*

Fr combien coûtent les places ? *KON-byAN koot lay plass?*

Ger was kosten die Karten? *vas **kos**-tuhn dee **kahr**-tuhn?*

Gr πόσο κοστίζουν τα εισιτήρια; *po-so ko-**sti**-zoon ta i-si-**ti**-ri-a?*

It quanto costano i biglietti? *kwan-toh **kos**-ta-noh ee bee-**lyet**-tee?*

Por quanto custam os bilhetes? *kwahn-too **koosh**-touŋ oosh beel-**yae**-tesh?*

Sp ¿cuánto cuestan las entradas? *kwan-toh **kwes**-tan las en-**trah**-das?*

Swe hur mycket kostar en biljett? *hoor **muk**-eh **kost**-ar en bil-**yet**?*

Culture Vultures

124

Fun fact!

In countries where English-language films are routinely dubbed, like **France** and **Spain**, the stars have their own personal dubber who provides the voice for all their work.

I'd like to go and see a play/a show

Cz rád (m)/ráda (f) bych se šel (m)/šla (f) podívat na nějakou hru/nějaké představení *r<u>a</u>d/**r<u>a</u>d**-a beekh se shel/shla **po**-<u>deev</u>-at na nye-ya-ko-oo hroo/nye-ya-k<u>e</u> **przhed**-stav-en-<u>ee</u>*

Dan jeg vil gerne se et teaterstykke/en forestilling *yai vil gern seh eht teh-**ah**-tuhr-stue-kuh/ehn **for**-ruh-stil-ling*

Dut ik zou graag naar een toneelstuk/voorstelling gaan *ik zow CHrahCH nahr en toh-**nayl**-stek/**for**-stel-ing CHahn*

Fr j'aimerais bien aller voir une pièce/un spectacle *zhem-ray byAN a-lay vwar Un pyess/AN spek-takl*

Ger ich hätte Lust, ein Teaterstück/eine Show zu sehen *ish het-uh lust, eyn tay-**ah**-tuh-stuuk/**ey**-ne shoh tsoo **zay**-uhn*

Gr θα ήθελα να δω μία παράσταση/ένα θέαμα *THa i-THe-la na tho **mi**-a pa-**ra**-sta-si/**e**-na **THe**-a-ma*

It mi piacerebbe andare a vedere una commedia/uno spettacolo *mee pya-cher-**eb**-bay an-**dah**-ray a vay-**day**-ray **oo**-na kom-**may**-dee-a/**oo**-noh spet-**ta**-koh-loh*

125

Por	gostaria de ver uma peça de teatro/ir a um espectáculo *goosh-tUH-ree-UH dae vaer oo-mUH peh-sUH dae tee-ah-troo/eer UH oom esh-peh-tah-koo-loo*
Sp	me gustaría ir a ver una obra de teatro/una actuación *may goos-ta-ree-a eer a bair oo-na ob-ra day tay-ah-troh/oo-na ak-too-ath-yohn*
Swe	jag skulle vilja gå och se en pjäs/en show *yahg skool-eh vil-ya gaw och see en pee-ais/en show*

I'd like to go to the ballet/the opera

Cz	rád (m)/ráda (f) bych šel (m)/šla (f) na balet/na operu *rad/rad-a beekh shel/shla na bal-et/na op-er-oo*
Dan	jeg vil gerne i balletten/operaen *yai vil gern ee ba-lett-uhn/o-puh-raa-uhn*
Dut	ik zou graag naar het ballet/de opera gaan *ik zow CHrahCH nahr het ba-lay/de op-er-a CHahn*
Fr	j'aimerais bien aller voir un ballet/aller à l'opéra *zhem-ray byAN a-lay vwar AN ba-lay/a-lay a lop-ay-ra*
Ger	ich hätte Lust ins Ballett/in die Oper zu gehen *ish het-uh lust ins ba-let/in dee oh-puh tsoo gay-uhn*
Gr	θα ήθελα να πάω σε μια παράσταση μπαλέτου/στην όπερα *THa i-THe-la na pa-o se mi-a pa-ra-sta-si ba-le-too/stin o-pe-ra*
It	mi piacerebbe andare a vedere un balletto/un'opera lirica *mee pee-ah-cher-eb-bay an-dah-ray a vay-day-ray oon bal-let-toh/oon-o-pay-ra lee-ree-ka*
Por	gostaria de ver um bailado/ir à ópera *goosh-tUH-ree-UH dae vaer oom ba-ee-lah-doo/eer ah oh-pae-rUH*
Sp	me gustaría ir al ballet/a la ópera *may goos-ta-ree-a eer al ba-let/a la op-air-a*
Swe	jag skulle gilla att gå på balett/opera *yahg skool-eh yill-a att gaw paw ba-lett/oo-per-a*

that was great/pretty boring

Cz	bylo to skvělý/byla to pěkná nuda *beel-o to skvyel-<u>ee</u>/beel-a to pyek-n<u>a</u> nood-a*
Dan	det var godt/temmeligt kedeligt *deh vaar gott/**teh**-muh-leet ke**TH**-uh-litt*
Dut	dat was geweldig/saai *dat vas CHe-**veld**-eCH/seye*
Fr	c'était super/plutôt ennuyeux *set-ay sU-pair/plU-toh on-wee-yuh*
Ger	das war toll/ziemlich langweilig *das var tol/**tseem**-liCH **lang**-vey-lish*
Gr	ήταν υπέροχο/βαρετό *i-tan i-**pe**-ro-ho/va-re-**to***
It	è stato fantastico/piuttosto noioso *ay stah-toh fan-**tas**-tee-koh/pyoo-**tos**-toh noy-**oh**-zoh*
Por	gostei muito/achei uma seca *goosh-**tay** mooy-too/U**H**-**shay** oo-mUH seh-kUH*
Sp	ha estado muy bien/bastante aburrida *a es-**tah**-doh mwee byen/bas-**tan**-tay a-boo-**RRee**-da*
Swe	det var härligt/ganska tråkigt *det vahr **hair**-ligt/**gan**-ska **traw**-kigt*

Fun fact!

The ancient **Greeks** were great fans of the theatre: in fact, the words drama, theatre, comedy and tragedy are all of Greek origin.

Culture Vultures

127

Listen up!

it starts at ...

Cz	začíná to v ... *zach-een-a to v ...*
Dan	det starter klokken ... *deh staa-tuhr kloh-kuhn ...*
Dut	het begint om... *het be-CHint om ...*
Fr	ça commence à ... *sa ko-mONs a ...*
Ger	es beginnt um ... *ess buh-gint um ...*
Gr	αρχίζει στις ... *ar-hi-zi stis ...*
It	comincia alle ... *ko-meen-cha al-lay ...*
Por	começa às ... *koo-meh-sUH ahs ...*
Sp	empieza a la ... *em-pyay-tha a las ...*
Swe	det börjar klockan ... *det bur-yar klok-an ...*

it's sold out

Cz	je to vyprodané *ye to vee-prod-an-e*
Dan	der er udsolgt *dehr ehr ooTH-solt*
Dut	het is uitverkocht *het is euit-fer-koCHt*
Fr	c'est complet *say kom-play*
Ger	es ist ausverkauft *ess ist ows-fehr-kowft*
Gr	τα εισιτήρια έχουν εξαντληθεί *ta i-si-ti-ri-a e-hoon e-xan-dli-THi*
It	non ci sono più posti *non chee so-noh pyoo pos-tee*
Por	está esgotado *esh-tah ezh-goo-tah-doo*
Sp	no hay entradas *noh eye en-trah-das*
Swe	det är utsålt *det air oot-solt*

where would you like to sit?

Cz	kam to chcete? *kam to khtset-e?*
Dan	hvor vil du gerne sidde henne? *vor vil doo gern si-THuh he-nuh?*
Dut	waar zou je willen zitten? *vahr zow je vil-e(n) zit-e(n)?*
Fr	où voulez-vous être placé ? *oo voo-lay voo etr pla-say?*
Ger	wo möchten Sie gerne sitzen? *voh meush-tuhn zee gehr-nuh zit-suhn?*

Culture Vultures

Gr	πού θα ήθελες να καθήσεις; *poo THa i-THe-les na ka-THi-sis?*
It	quali posti desiderate? *kwah-lee pos-tee day-zee-day-rah-tay?*
Por	onde quer sentar-se? *ond kehr sain-tahr-sae?*
Sp	¿dónde se quiere sentar? *don-day say kyair-ay sen-tar?*
Swe	var vill ni sitta? *vahr vill nee sitt-a?*

please turn off your mobile phones

Cz	vypněte si, prosím, své mobilní telefony *veep-nye-te see, pro-seem, sve mob-eel-nee tel-ef-on-ee*
Dan	vær venlig at slukke for mobiltelefoner *vehr ven-lee att sluh-kuh for mob-eel-te-le-fon-uh*
Dut	gelieve uw mobiele telefoon uit te zetten *CHe-leev-e oo mob-eel-e tehl-e-fohn euit te zet-e(n)*
Fr	prière d'éteindre votre portable *pree-air day-tANdr votr por-tahbl*
Ger	bitte schalten Sie Ihre Handy aus *bit-uh shal-tuhn zee ee-ruh hen-dee ows*
Gr	παρακαλείσθε να απενεργοποιήσετε τα κινητά σας *pa-ra-ka-lis-THe na a-pe-ner-gho-pi-i-se-te ta ki-ni-ta sas*
It	si prega di spegnere i telefoni cellulari *see pray-ga dee spen-yer-ay ee tay-le-fo-nee chel-loo-lah-ree*
Por	é favor de desligar os telemóveis *eh fUH-vor dae daesh-lee-gahr oosh teh-leh-moh-vaysh*
Sp	por favor apaguen sus teléfonos móviles *por fa-bor a-pa-gen soos te-lay-fo-nohs mob-ee-lays*
Swe	vänligen stäng av mobiltelefonerna *vain-lig-en steng av mob-eel-tel-eh-foon-er-na*

Fun fact!

One of **Sweden**'s favourite 'cultural' events is the Eurovision Song Contest, which is taken very seriously indeed: the country is still proud of bringing Abba to the world in 1974, when they won the contest with 'Waterloo'!

♥ The Language of Love ♥

do you come here often?

Cz chodíš sem často?
khod-<u>ee</u>sh sem chas-to?

Dan kommer du her ofte?
kom-muhr doo hehr oft-tuh?

Dut kom je hier vaker?
kom ye heer fah-ker?

Fr tu viens souvent ici ?
tU vyAN soo-vON ee-see?

Ger kommst du öfters hierher?
komst doo euf-tuhs heer-hehr?

Gr έρχεσαι εδώ συχνά;
er-he-se eth-o sih-na?

It vieni qui spesso?
*vee-**ay**-nee kwee **spess**-oh?*

Por vem aqui muitas vezes?
*vaim UH-**kee** **mooy**-tUHsh **vae**-zesh?*

Sp ¿vienes mucho por aquí?
***byen**-es **moo**-choh por a-**kee**?*

Swe kommer du ofta hit?
***komm**-er doo **off**-ta hit?*

Music, Moshpits and Mud

Vital Vocab

band

Cz	skupina *skoo-pee-na*, kapela *kap-e-la*
Dan	band *band*
Dut	band *behnt*
Fr	groupe *groop*
Ger	Gruppe *grup-uh*, Band *bend*
Gr	γκρούπ *groop*
It	gruppo *groop-poh*
Por	banda *bUHn-dUH*, grupo *groo-poo*
Sp	grupo *groo-poh*
Swe	band *band*

concert

Cz	koncert *kon-tsert*
Dan	koncert *kon-sehrt*
Dut	concert *kon-sehrt*
Fr	concert *kON-sair*
Ger	Konzert *kon-tsehrt*
Gr	κονσέρτο *kon-ser-to*
It	concerto *kon-cher-toh*
Por	concerto *kon-saer-too*
Sp	concierto *kon-thyair-toh*
Swe	konsert *kon-sert*

festival

Cz	festival	*fes-tee-val*
Dan	festival	*fes-tee-val*
Dut	festival	*fehs-ti-val*
Fr	festival	*fes-tee-val*
Ger	Festival	*fes-ti-vel*
Gr	φεστιβάλ	*fes-ti-val*
It	festival	*fes-tee-val*
Por	festival	*faesh-tee-vahl*
Sp	festival	*fes-tee-bahl*
Swe	festival	*fes-ti-vahl*

In the Know

Although concerts and events take place all year round, it's during the summer months that Europe really comes alive with the sound of music. One of the biggest and best-known music festivals is **Roskilde** in Denmark, held every summer since 1971 and on a similar scale to Britain's Glastonbury with a huge line-up of major rock and pop acts. Tickets include about a week's camping and are sold all over Europe – visit **www.roskilde-festival.dk** to find your nearest vendor. Roskilde's southern rival is Spain's **Benicassim**, held every summer near Valencia. This festival plays host to both big-name and alternative acts: most perform late in the day when it's a bit cooler, so you can spend your days on the nearby beach. Germany hosts **Rock am Ring** every summer at the Nürburgring race track near Koblenz, featuring mainly well-known rock acts plus camping facilities. Its sister festival, **Rock im Park**, has been held in Nuremberg since 1993. Also in Germany, dance and techno fans can enjoy the July **Love Parade** in Berlin, a giant street party extending into special club nights and raves.

Les Eurockéennes de Belfort is an outdoor rock and pop festival held every summer in eastern France, while the Netherlands has the annual **Pinkpop** festival in the south of the country (the name comes

Music, Mosh Pits and Mud

from the Dutch **Pinksteren** meaning Pentecost, the weekend it's held, rather than any 'gay' connotations). Portugal's biggest summer festival is **Super Bock Super Rock** (sponsored by the popular Super Bock lager), held in Lisbon and attracting well-known rock and pop acts. Day tickets and three-day camping passes are available. **Rock in Rio** was originally held in Brazil but now comes to Lisbon every two years: this festival has a charity function as well as featuring well-known rock, pop and dance acts. In Sweden, the **Uppsala Reggae Festival** in August draws big crowds, or head to Skansen on Midsummer's Eve (a major celebration for Swedes) for a huge outdoor event with both traditional and modern music and dancing. The following day is a national holiday so the schnapps flows freely! In the Czech Republic, the biggest summer music event is **Rock for People** in Český Brod, featuring Czech and European acts alongside better-known ones. Alternatively, try **Hip Hop Kemp** in Hradec Králové, an underground festival with very cheap camping, or the **United Islands of Prague** (a world music event spread over three islands in the Vltava river).

Many other smaller and more specialised events are held all over Europe throughout the year. Of course, big international stars tend to only perform in major cities, but look out for interesting local acts and small festivals: check the local guides, pick up flyers in bars and clubs or ask around. And try to sample the local culture too: from German folk music to Spanish flamenco, most countries have their own musical tradition. Portuguese fado is a type of sad, nostalgic singing accompanied by a guitar – visit a **casa de fado** (fado house) where you can have a meal and enjoy the music. As with most traditional culture, performances are laid on for tourists – for a more authentic version, try the bars in the Alfama district of Lisbon where several modern fado singers started out.

Fun fact!

The first **Rock In Rio** took place in 1985, attracting over 1.3 million people in ten days (equivalent to five Wood-stocks!) and starring the likes of Queen and Rod Stewart alongside Brazilian acts. In 1991 it took over Rio's Maracanã stadium, and in 2001 got its own purpose-built 'City of Rock'. The festival's slogan is 'For A Better World': proceeds go to Brazilian and **Portuguese** youth charities.

Over to you

what sort of music are you into?

Cz   jaký druh muziky se ti líbí? *yak-ee drookh mooz-eek-ee se tee leeb-ee?*

Dan   hvilken slags musik kan du lide? *vil-kuhn slahks mu-seek kan doo lee?*

Dut   van wat voor soort muziek houd je? *fan vat for sohrt moo-zeek how ye?*

Fr   quel genre de musique tu écoutes ? *kel zhONr duh mU-zeek tU ay-koot?*

Ger   was hörst du so für Musik? *vas heurst doo soh fuur moo-zeek?*

Gr	τι μουσική σου αρέσει; *ti moo-si-ki soo a-re-si?*
It	che musica ti piace? *kay **moo**-zee-ka tee pee-**ah**-chay?*
Por	de que género de música gosta? *dae kae **zhaen**-roo dae **moo**-zee-kUH gosh-tUH?*
Sp	¿qué tipo de música te gusta? *kay **tee**-poh day **moo**-see-ka tay **goos**-ta?*
Swe	vilken sorts musik gillar du? *vil-ken sorts moo-**seek** yill-ar doo?*

I like rap/R & B/rock/dance/jazz

Cz	mám rád rap/R & B/rock/dance music/jazz *m<u>a</u>m r<u>a</u>d rap/**ar**-n-bee/rock/dans **mooz**-eek/dzhes*
Dan	jeg kan godt lide rap/R & B/rock/dance/jazz *yai kan gott lee rap/ar-n-bee/rok/dans/jazz*
Dut	ik houd van rap/R & B/rock/dance/jazz *ik how van rehp/ehr en bay/rok/dans/jehz*
Fr	j'aime bien le rap/le R&B/le rock/la dance/le jazz *zhem byAN luh rap/luh ar-n-bee/le rok/la dans/le jaz*
Ger	ich mag gern Rap/R & B/Rock/Dance/Jazz *ish mahg gehrn rep/ar-n-**bee**/rok/dents/jez*
Gr	μου αρέσει η ραπ/ριθμ εντ μπλουζ/ροκ/χορευτική/τζαζ *moo a-**re**-si i rap/**ri**-THm end blooz/rok/ho-re-fti-**ki**/tzaz*
It	mi piace il rap/il rhythm'n blues/il rock/la musica dance/il jazz *mee pee-**ah**-chay eel rap/eel **reet**-am an blooz/eel rok/la **moo**-zee-ka dayns/eel jayts*
Por	gosto de rap/R & B/rock/dance/jazz *gosh-too dae RRap/ahr-n-bee/rok/dans/jazz*
Sp	me gusta el rap/el R & B/el rock/la música dance/el jazz *may **goos**-ta el rap/el ar-en-**bee**/el rok/la **moo**-see-ka dans/el jazz*
Swe	jag gillar rap/R & B/rock/dans/jazz *yahg **yill**-ar/rap/ahr-n-**bee**/rok/dans/yazz*

my favourite band/singer is ...

Cz moje oblíbená kapela *(band)*/můj oblíbený zpěvák *(male singer)*/ moje oblíbená zpěvačka *(female singer)* je ... *moy-e ob-leeb-en-a kap-e-la/moo-y ob-leeb-enee zpyev-ak/moy-e ob-leeb-en-a zpyev-ach-ka ye ...*

Dan mit ynglingsband/sanger er ... *meet ueng-lings-band/saang-uh ehr ...*

Dut mijn favoriete band/zanger is ... *mayn fav-or-eet-e behnt/zang-er is ...*

Fr mon groupe préféré *(band)*/mon chanteur préféré *(male singer)*/ ma chanteuse préférée *(female singer)*, c'est... *mON groop pray-fair-ay/mON shON-tuhr pray-fair-ay/ma shON-tuhz pray-fair-ay, say ...*

Ger meine Lieblingsband *(band)*/mein Lieblingssänger *(male singer)*/meine Lieblingssängerin *(female singer)* ist ... *mey-nuh leep-lingz-bend/meyn leep-lingz-seng-uh/mey-nuh leep-lingz-seng-uh-rin ist ...*

Gr το αγαπημένο μου γκρουπ *(band)*/ο αγαπημένος μου τραγουδιστής *(male singer)*/η αγαπημένη μου τραγουδίστρια *(female singer)* είναι ... *to a-gha-pi-me-no moo groop/o a-gha-pi-me-nos moo tra-ghoo-thi-stis/i a-gha-pi-me-ni moo tra-ghoo-thi-stri-a i-ne ...*

It il mio gruppo/cantante preferito è ... *eel mee-oh groop-poh/kan-tan-tay pray-fay-ree-toh ay ...*

Por o meu grupo favorito *(band)*/o meu cantor favorito *(male singer)*/a minha cantora favorita *(female singer)* é ... *oo may-oo groo-poo fUH-voo-ree-too/oo may-oo kan-tor fUH-voo-ree-too/UH meen-yUH kan-toh-rUH fUH-voo-ree-tUH eh ...*

Sp mi grupo/cantante preferido es ... *mee groo-poh/kan-tan-tay pref-air-ee-doh es ...*

Swe mitt favoritband/min favoritartist är ... *mitt fav-oor-eet-band/min fav-or-eet-art-ist air ...*

Fun fact!

On 21 June (Midsummer's Eve), the whole of **France** celebrates **la Fête de la musique** (the music festival). From big cities to the smallest villages, amateur and professional musicians can play wherever they want at any time of day or night, totalling some 1500 free concerts!

are there any free concerts?

Cz	jsou tu nějaké koncerty s bezplatným vstupem? *yso-oo tad-ee nye-yak-e kon-tsert-ee s bez-plat-neem vstoop-em?*
Dan	er der nogen gratiskoncerter? *ehr dehr no-wuhn graa-tees-kon-sehr-tuh?*
Dut	zijn er gratis concerten? *zayn her CHrat-is kon-sehrt-e(n)?*
Fr	est-ce qu'il y a des concerts gratuits ? *ess keel ya day kON-sair gra-twee?*
Ger	gibt es irgendwelche kostenlosen Konzerte? *geept ess eer-guhnd-vel-shuh kos-tuhn-lohz-uhn kon-tsehr-tuh?*
Gr	υπάρχουν συναυλίες με ελεύθερη είσοδο; *i-par-hoon si-na-vli-es me e-le-fTHe-ri i-so-tho?*
It	ci sono concerti gratuiti? *chee so-noh kon-cher-tee gra-too-ee-tee?*
Por	há algum concerto de graça? *ah al-goom kon-saer-too dae grah-sUH?*

Sp	¿hay conciertos gratis? *eye kon-thyair-tohs grah-tees?*
Swe	finns det några gratis konserter? *finns det naw-gra grah-tis kon-sert-er?*

are there any bars with live music?

Cz	jsou tu nějaké bary s živou hudbou? *yso-oo too nye-yak-e bar-ee s zheev-o-oo hood-bo-oo?*
Dan	er der nogen barer med livemusik? *ehr dehr no-wuhn bah-uh meTH laiv-mu-seek?*
Dut	zijn er café's met live muziek? *zayn ehr kaf-ays meht leyev moo-zeek?*
Fr	est-ce qu'il y a des bars avec de la musique live ? *ess keel ya day bar a-vek duh la mU-zeek leyv?*
Ger	gibt es irgendwelche Bars mit Live-Musik? *geept ess eer-guhnd-vel-shuh bars mit leyf-moo-zeek?*
Gr	υπάρχουν κέντρα με ζωντανή μουσική; *i-par-hoon ken-dra me zon-da-ni moo-si-ki?*
It	ci sono locali con musica dal vivo? *chee so-noh lo-kah-lee kon moo-zee-ka dal vee-voh?*
Por	há algum bar com música ao vivo? *ah al-goom bahr kom moo-zee-kUH ow vee-voo?*
Sp	¿hay bares con música en vivo? *eye bar-ays kon moo-see-ka en bee-boh?*
Swe	finns det någon bar med live musik? *finns det naw-gon bahr med live moo-seek?*

Fun fact!

The word **festival** in **Italian** also means 'song contest', and these events are popular with young people. The most famous are the **San Remo Festival** and the open-air **Festivalbar**, held in a different place every year.

it was a fantastic gig

Cz   to bylo super *to beel-o soop-er*

Dan det var en fantastisk koncert *deh vaar ehn fan-tas-tisk kon-sehrt*

Dut het was een fantastisch optreden *het vas en fan-tas-tis op-trayd-e(n)*

Fr   c'était un concert génial *set-ay AN kON-sair zhay-nyal*

Ger das war 'ne super Mucke *das var nuh zoo-puh muk-uh*

Gr   ήταν ένα φανταστικό μουσικό συμβάν *i-tan e-na fan-da-sti-ko moo-si-ko sim-van*

It   è stato un concerto fantastico *ay stah-toh oon kon-cher-toh fan-tas-tee-koh*

Por foi um espectáculo fantástico *foy oom esh-peh-tah-koo-loo fan-tahsh-tee-koo*

Sp   ha sido un concierto alucinante *a see-doh oon kon-thyair-toh a-loo-thee-nan-tay*

Swe det var en fantastisk spelning *det vahr en fan-tas-tisk speel-ning*

I'm not really into that sort of music

Cz tenhle druh muziky mě moc nebere *ten-hle drookh* **mooz**-*eek-ee*
    mye mots **ne**-*ber-e*

Dan jeg er ikke så meget til den slags musik *yai ehr* **ik**-*kuh saw* **mai**-
    *yuht til dehn slahks mu-***seek**

Dut ik houd niet zo van dat soort muziek *ik how neet zoh van dat*
    *sohrt moo-***zeek**

Fr je n'aime pas trop ce genre de musique *zhuh nem pa troh suh*
    zhONr duh mU-zeek

Ger ich mag solche Musik nicht so wahnsinnig *ish mahg* **sol**-*shuh*
    *moo-***zeek** *nisht soh* **vahn**-*zin-ish*

Gr δεν μου αρέσει πραγματικά αυτό το είδος μουσικής *then moo*
    *a-***re**-*si pra-ghma-ti-***ka** *af-***to** *to i-thos moo-si-***kis**

It non è proprio il mio genere di musica preferito *non ay* **prop**-*ree-*
    oh eel **mee**-*oh* **gen**-*ay-ray dee* **moo**-*zee-ka pray-fay-***ree**-*toh*

Por não é o meu género de música *noun eh oo* **may**-*oo* **zhehn**-*roo*
    dae **moo**-*zee-kUH*

Sp no me gusta mucho ese tipo de música *noh may* **goos**-*ta moo-*
    choh **es**-*ay* **tee**-*poh day* **moo**-*see-ka*

Swe jag tycker inte speciellt om den sortens musik *yahg* **tuk**-*er in-*
    *teh spe-si-***elt** *om den* **sort**-*ens moo-***seek**

I've seen them before, they're brilliant live

Cz už jsem je viděl dřív, naživo jsou skvělý *oozh y***sem** *ye* **veed**-*yel*
    drzh<u>eev</u>, **na**-*zheev-o y***so**-*oo* <u>skvyel</u>-<u>ee</u>

Dan jeg har set dem før, de er fantastiske live *yai haar seht dem foer,*
    *dee ehr fan-***tas**-*tis-kuh laiv*

Dut ik heb ze eerder gezien, ze zijn geweldig live *ik hehp ze* **ayr**-*der*
    *CHe-***zeen**, *ze zayn CHe-***veld**-*eCH leyev*

Fr je les ai déjà vus avant, ils sont super en concert *zhuh layz ay*
    day-zha vU a-vON, eel sON sU-pair ON kON-sair

Ger ich hab die schonmal gesehen, die sind live echt klasse *ish*
    hahb dee **shohn**-*mahl guh-***zay**-*uhn, dee zint leyf eCHt* **klas**-*uh*

141

Gr	τους έχω ξαναδεί, δίνουν πολύ ωραίες συναυλίες *toos e-ho xa-na-thi, thi-noon po-li o-re-es si-na-vli-es*
It	li ho già visti, sono fortissimi dal vivo *lee oh ja vees-tee, so-noh for-tees-see-mee dal vee-voh*
Por	já os vi antes, são fantásticos ao vivo *zhah oosh vee UHn-tesh, souɳ fan-tahsh-tee-koosh ow vee-voo*
Sp	ya los he visto antes, son buenísimos en vivo *ya los ay bees-toh an-tays, son bwen-ees-ee-mohs en bee-boh*
Swe	jag har sett dem förut, de är lysande live *yahg hahr sett dom fur-oot, dom air loos-an-deh live*

Fun fact!

Denmark's **Roskilde** festival has a unique tradition: every year, there is a 'naked race' for nude runners of both sexes, the prize being tickets to the following year's event!

we're here for the ... festival

Cz	přijeli jsme sem na ... festival *przhee-yel-ee ysme sem na ... fest-ee-val*
Dan	vi er her på grund af ...festivallen *vee ehr hehr paw groen a ... fes-ti-val-luhn*
Dut	we zijn hier voor het ...festival *ve zayn heer for het ... fehs-ti-val*
Fr	on est là pour le festival de ... *on ay la poor luh fes-tee-val duh ...*

Ger	wir sind wegen des ...-Festivals gekommen *veer sint **vay**-guhn des ...-**fes**-ti-vels guh-**kom**-uhn*
Gr	είμαστε εδώ για το φεστιβάλ ... *i-ma-ste e-**tho** ya to fe-sti-**val** ...*
It	siamo venuti per il festival (di) ... *see-**ah**-moh vay-**noo**-tee per eel **fes**-tee-val (dee) ...*
Por	viemos ao festival de ... *vee-**eh**-mooz ow faesh-tee-**vahl** dae ...*
Sp	hemos venido al festival ... ***ay**-mos ben-**ee**-doh al fes-tee-**bahl** ...*
Swe	vi är här för att gå på ... festivalen *vee air hair fur att gaw paw ... fest-i-**vahl**-en*

what bands are playing?

Cz	jaké kapely hrajou? *yak-**e** **kap**-el-ee **hraj**-o-oo?*
Dan	hvilke bands er det, der spiller? *vil-kuh bands ehr deh, dehr **spill**-uh?*
Dut	welke bands treden op? *vehl-ke behnds **trayd**-e(n) op?*
Fr	quels sont les groupes qui jouent ? *kel sON lay groop kee zhoo?*
Ger	welche Bands treten auf? *vel-shuh bends **tray**-tuhn owf?*
Gr	ποιά γκρουπ παίζουν; *pi-**a** groop **pe**-zoon?*
It	che gruppi suonano? *kay **groop**-pee soo-**oh**-na-noh?*
Por	quais são os grupos que vão actuar? *kwa-eesh souŋ oosh **groo**-poosh kae vouŋ UH-too-**ahr**?*
Sp	¿qué grupos tocan? *kay **groo**-pohs **toh**-kan?*
Swe	vilka band spelar? *vil-ka band **spee**-lar?*

where can we pitch our tent?

Cz	kde si můžem postavit stan? *kde see **moozh**-em **post**-av-eet stan?*
Dan	hvor må vi sætte vores telt op? *vor maw vee **seht**-tuh vors tehlt op?*
Dut	waar kunnen we onze tent opzetten? *vahr **ken**-e(n) ve **on**-ze tehnt **op**-zeht-e(n)?*
Fr	où est-ce qu'on peut planter notre tente ? *oo ess kON puh plON-tay notr tONt?*
Ger	wo können wir unser Zelt aufbauen? *voh **keun**-uhn veer **un**-zuh tselt **owf**-bow-uhn?*

143

Gr	πού μπορούμε να στήσουμε την σκηνή μας; *poo bo-roo-me na sti-soo-me tin ski-ni mas?*
It	dove possiamo piantare la tenda? *doh-vay pos-see-ah-moh pee-an-tah-ray la ten-da?*
Por	onde pudemos montar a tenda? *ond poo-day-moosh mon-tahr UH tain-dUH?*
Sp	¿dónde podemos montar la tienda? *don-day po-day-mos mon-tar la tyen-da?*
Swe	var kan vi sätta upp vårt tält? *vahr kan vee sett-a oop vawrt telt?*

is there a bar?

Cz	je tam bar? *ye tam bar?*
Dan	er der en bar? *ehr dehr ehn bah?*
Dut	is er een bar? *is ehr en bar?*
Fr	est-ce qu'il y a un bar ? *ess keel ya AN bar?*
Ger	gibt es hier eine Bar? *geept ess heer ey-nuh bar?*
Gr	υπάρχει κανένα μπαρ; *i-pa-rhi ka-ne-na bar?*
It	c'è un bar? *chay oon bar?*
Por	há algum bar? *ah al-goom bahr?*
Sp	¿hay bar? *eye bar?*
Swe	finns det någon bar? *finns det naw-gon bahr?*

where are the toilets, please?

Cz	prosím vás, kde jsou toalety? *pro-seem vas, kde yso-oo to-a-le-tee?*
Dan	undskyld, hvor er toilettet? *uhn-skuel, vor ehr toi-lett-uht?*
Dut	waar is het toilet, alstublieft? *vahr is het twa-leht, als-too-bleeft?*
Fr	où sont les toilettes, s'il vous plaît ? *oo sON lay twa-let, seel voo play?*
Ger	wo sind denn hier die Toiletten, bitte? *voh zint den heer dee twa-let-uhn, bit-uh?*
Gr	πού είναι οι τουαλέτες, παρακαλώ; *poo i-ne i too-a-le-tes, pa-ra-ka-lo?*
It	dov'è la toilette, per favore? *doh-vay la twa-let, per fa-vor-ay?*

144

Por por favor, onde são as casas-de-banho? *poor fUH-vor, on-d soun UHsh kah-zUHsh dae bUHn-yoo?*

Sp ¿dónde están los baños, por favor? *don-day es-tan los ban-yohs, por fa-bor?*

Swe var finns toaletten? *vahr finns too-lett-en?*

♥ The Language of Love ♥

I've just arrived at the festival, can you give me directions to your tent?

Cz právě jsem přijel *(m)*/přijela *(f)* na festival, můžeš mi ukázat cestu k tvému stanu?
prav-ye ysem przhee-yel/przhee-yel-a na fest-ee-val, moozh-esh mee oo-kaz-at tsest-oo k tvem-oo stan-oo?

Dan jeg er lige ankommet til festivallen, kan du ikke sige mig vejen hen til dit telt?
yai ehr lee an-kom-muht til fes-ti-val-luhn, kan doo ik-kuh see mai vai-yuhn hehn til deet tehlt?

Dut ik ben net aangekomen op het festival, kun je me vertellen hoe ik bij jouw tent kan komen?
ik behn neht ahn-CHe-kohm-e(n) op het fehs-ti-val, ken ye me fer-tehl-e(n) hoo ik bay jow tehnt kan kohm-e(n)?

Fr je viens d'arriver au festival, est-ce que tu pourrais m'indiquer le chemin jusqu'à ta tente ?
zhuh vyAN da-ree-vay oh fes-tee-val, ess-kuh tU poo-ray mAN-dee-kay luh shuh-mAN zhUs-ka ta tONt?

Ger ich bin grad erst angekommen, kannst du mir vielleicht sagen wo dein Zelt ist?
ish bin grahd ehrst an-guh-kom-uhn, kanst doo meer vee-leyCHt zah-guhn voh deyn tselt ist?

Music, Moshpits and Mud

Gr μόλις έφτασα στο φεστιβάλ, μπορείς να μου δείξεις πού είναι η σκηνή σου;

mo-lis e-fta-sa sto fe-sti-val, bo-ris na moo thi-xis poo i-ne i ski-ni soo?

It sono appena arrivato al festival: mi potresti indicare dove si trova la tua tenda?

so-noh ap-pay-na ar-ree-vah-to al fes-tee-val: mee pot-res-tee een-dee-kah-ray dov-ay see troh-va la too-a ten-da?

Por acabei de chegar ao festival, pode-me indicar a sua tenda?

UH-kUH-bay dae shae-gahr ow faesh-tee-vahl, pod-mae een-dee-kahr UH soo-UH tain-dUH?

Sp acabo de llegar al festival, ¿me dices cómo llegar a tu tienda?

a-kah-boh day yay-gar al fes-tee-bahl, may dee-thes kom-oh yay-gar a too tyen-da?

Swe jag har just kommit till festivalen, kan du berätta mig vägen till ditt tält?

yahg hah yoost komm-it till fest-i-vahl-en, kan doo bee-rett-a may vaig-en till dit telt?

Let Me Entertain You

Vital vocab

party

Cz	večírek *vech-<u>ee</u>-rek*, party *par-tee*
Dan	fest *fest*
Dut	feest *fayst*
Fr	fête *fet*
Ger	Party *par-ty*
Gr	γιορτή *yor-ti*, πάρτυ *par-ti*
It	festa *fes-ta*
Por	festa *fehsh-tUH*
Sp	fiesta *fyes-ta*
Swe	fest *fest*

to have a party

Cz	pořádat večírek/party *po-rzh<u>a</u>d-at vech-<u>ee</u>-rek/par-tee*
Dan	at holde fest *att hol fest*
Dut	een feest geven *en fayst CHay-ve(n)*
Fr	faire une fête *fair Un fet*
Ger	eine Party schmeißen *ey-nuh par-ty shmey-suhn*
Gr	γιορτάζω/κάνω πάρτυ *yor-ta-zo/ka-no par-ti*
It	dare una festa *dah-ray oo-na fes-ta*
Por	dar/fazer uma festa *dahr/fUH-zaer oo-mUH fehsh-tUH*
Sp	hacer una fiesta *a-thair oo-na fyes-ta*
Swe	ha en fest *hah en fest*

147

In the Know

If you're lucky enough to be welcomed into the homes of your new-found friends, you'll find it's a great opportunity to meet people and learn about local customs. Entertaining at home is popular in Denmark and Sweden (perhaps due to the cold weather, or the high price of drinks in bars!). You should arrive on time (but not early) and even for informal events it's customary to bring a small gift such as flowers or a plant, a bottle of wine or something for the home like candles. The Czechs also enjoy entertaining; wine and home-made cakes are popular gifts. Like here, you should be punctual if invited to a sit-down dinner; parties are more relaxed and informal. House parties are popular in Germany: again, be punctual and bring some alcohol and/or snacks to share with the other guests (this little gift is known as a **Mitbringsel**).

Greeks and Italians are on the whole very hospitable and love having friends round for sociable meals – there's always some excuse for a celebration! Attitudes to punctuality are relaxed and they will usually give a vague time of arrival. Bring the usual gifts and an empty stomach, as meals tend to be copious and your hosts will have gone to some trouble! The French are also known for their good food and like to entertain at home. Students and young people often have friends round for an informal meal; if invited it's polite to ask if you can bring anything, such as a dessert. Alternatively, you might just be invited for drinks and nibbles – young people always appreciate it if you bring a bottle, while for older people flowers and chocolates are common gifts.

In Spain and Portugal it's more common to meet friends in a bar or restaurant; however people do sometimes get together for an informal meal at home. It's polite to take your host a small gift (in Portugal, this would usually be chocolates or flowers rather than wine). If you're going to a house party organized by young people, you should take something to drink (beer and spirits are more common than wine). Bear in mind that most countries don't share the British drinking culture and not every social gathering is a boozy affair – the best plan is just to do as your hosts do!

Remember that people will be interested in you and your culture, and will be delighted with any traditional gifts you can bring from home. Plus some unfamiliar food always makes a good talking point!

Listen up!

come round to mine for drinks before we go out

Cz zastav se u mě pro pití, než vyrazíme *za-stav se oo* mnye **pro** pee-*tee*, nezh **vee**-raz-*ee*-me

Dan vi kan drikke hos mig, før vi går ud *vee kan* **dre**-*kuh hoss mai, foer vee gawr* ooTH

Dut kom bij mij iets drinken voor we uitgaan *kom bay may eets* **drink**-*e(n) for ve* **euit**-*CHahn*

Fr viens boire un verre chez moi avant qu'on sorte *vyAN bwar AN vair shay mwa a-vON kON sort*

Ger wir können bei mir noch etwas trinken, bevor wir losgehen *veer* **keun**-*uhn bey meer noCH* **et**-*vas* **tring**-*kuhn, be-***for** *veer* **lohs**-*gay-uhn*

Gr έλα από το σπίτι μου για ένα ποτό πριν βγούμε έξω *e-la a-***po** *to* **spi**-*ti moo ya* **e**-*na po-***to** *prin* **vghoo**-*me* **e**-*xo*

It vieni a bere qualcosa da me prima che usciamo *vee-***ay**-*nee a* **bay**-*ray kwal-***koh**-*za da may* **pree**-*ma kay oo-***shah**-*moh*

Por passe por minha casa para tomarmos um copo antes de sa-irmos *pass poor* **meen**-*yUH* **kah**-*zUH* **pUH**-*rUH too-***mahr**-*moosh oom* **koh**-*poo* **UHn**-*tsh dae* **sUH**-**eer**-*moosh*

Sp pásate por mi casa a tomar algo antes de salir *pas-a-tay por mee* **ka**-*sa a toh-***mar** *al-goh* **an**-*tes day sa-***leer**

Swe kom till mig på drink innan vi går ut *kom till may paw en drink* **inn**-*an vee gaw* **oot**

149

Fun fact!

In **France**, the **apéritif** or **apéro** is an informal social ritual. It's quite usual to be invited for pre-dinner drinks without the host actually providing dinner, or to meet friends in a café for an **apéritif** before going out for a meal.

I'm having a party tonight, would you like to come?

Cz   dneska večer pořádám party, přijdeš? *dnes-ka vech-er po-rzhad-am part-ee, przheed-esh?*

Dan   jeg holder fest i aften, har du ikke lyst til at komme? *yai hol-luhr fest ee aaf-tuhn, haar doo ik-kuh luest til att kom-muh?*

Dut   ik geef een feestje vanavond, heb je zin om te komen? *ik gayf en fayst-ye van-ah-vont, hehp ye zin om te kohm-e(n)?*

Fr   je fais une fête ce soir, tu veux venir ? *zhuh fay Un fet suh swar, tU vuh vuh-neer?*

Ger   bei mir ist heute Abend eine Party, hast du Lust zu kommen? *bey meer ist hoy-tuh ah-buhnt ey-nuh par-ty, hast doo lust tsoo kom-uhn?*

Gr   κάνω πάρτυ σήμερα το βράδυ, θα ήθελες να έρθεις; *ka-no par-ti si-me-ra to vra-thi, THa i-THe-les na er-THis?*

It   stasera do una festa, ti va di venire? *sta-say-ra do oo-na fes-ta, tee va dee vay-nee-ray?*

Por	vou dar uma festa hoje à noite, quer vir? *vo dahr oo-mUH fehsh-tUH ozh ah noy-t, kehr veer?*
Sp	hago una fiesta esta noche, ¿quieres venir? *a-goh oo-na fyes-ta es-ta no-chay, kyair-es ben-eer?*
Swe	jag ska ha fest ikväll, vill du komma? *yahg ska hah fest i-kvell, vil doo komm-a?*

why don't you come round for dinner one evening?

Cz	zastav se někdy večer na večeři! *za-stav se nye-kdee vech-er na vech-erzh-ee!*
Dan	har du lyst til at komme til middag hos mig? *haar doo luest til att kom-muh til me-dah hoss mai?*
Dut	waarom kom je niet eten 's avonds? *vahr-om kom ye neet ayt-e(n) sah-vonts?*
Fr	tu devrais venir dîner un soir ! *tU duh-vray vuh-neer dee-nay AN swar!*
Ger	wenn du magst, kannst du gern mal zum Abendessen vorbeikommen *ven doo mahgst, kanst doo gehrn mahl tsum ah-buhnt-ess-uhn vor-bey-kom-uhn*
Gr	γιατί δεν έρχεσαι να φάμε ένα βράδυ; *ya-ti then er-he-se na fa-me e-na vra-thi?*
It	perché non vieni a cena una di queste sere? *per-kay non vee-ay-nee a chay-na oo-na dee kwes-tay say-ray?*
Por	porque não vem jantar lá a casa um dia destes? *poor-kae nouŋ vaim zhUHn-tahr lah UH kah-zUH oom dee-ya daesh-taesh?*
Sp	¿por qué no te vienes a cenar un día a casa? *por kay noh tay byen-es a thay-nar oon dee-a a ka-sa?*
Swe	du kan väl komma på middag någon kväll? *doo kan vel komm-a paw mid-dahg naw-gon kvell?*

Fun fact!

In **Scandinavia**, **Germany** and the **Czech Republic**, it's customary to remove your shoes on entering someone's home. Czech hosts will usually provide you with a pair of slippers (**bačkory**).

Over to you

I've brought you a bottle of wine/some flowers

Cz	přinesl jsem ti láhev vína/nějaké květiny *przhee-nesl ysem tee lah-ev veen-a/nye-ya-ke kvyet-een-ee*
Dan	jeg har taget en flaske vin/nogle blomster med til dig *yai haar taht ehn flahs-kuh veen/no-wuhn blom-stuh meTH til dai*
Dut	ik heb een fles wijn/bloemen meegebracht *ik hehp en flehs vayn/bloom-e(n) may-CHe-braCHt*
Fr	j'ai apporté une bouteille de vin/des fleurs *zhay a-por-tay Un boo-tay duh vAN/day fluhr*
Ger	ich habe eine Flasche Wein/ein paar Blumen mitgebracht *ish hah-buh ey-nuh fla-shuh veyn/eyn pahr bloo-muhn mit-guh-braCHt*
Gr	σου έφερα ένα μπουκάλι κρασί/μερικά λουλούδια *soo e-fe-ra e-na boo-ka-li kra-si/me-ri-ka loo-loo-thi-a*

152

It	ti ho portato una bottiglia di vino/un mazzo di fiori *tee oh por-tah-to* **oo**-na bot-**tee**-lya dee **vee**-noh/oon **mat**-soh dee fee-**oh**-ree
Por	trouxe-lhe uma garrafa de vinho/um ramo de flores *trow-sae-lyee* oo-mUH gUH-**RRah**-fUH dae **veen**-yoo/oom RRUH-moo dae **flo**-raesh
Sp	te he traído una botella de vino/unas flores *tay ay tra-ee-doh* **oo**-na boh-**tel**-ya day **bee**-noh/oo-nas **flor**-ays
Swe	jag har med mig en flaska vin/blommor till dig *yahg hah med* may en **flas**-ka veen/**blomm**-or till day

Fun facts!

Flowers are always a popular gift when invited to someone's home, but choose carefully! Always give an odd number (not 13) in **Germany** and Eastern Europe – in the **Czech Republic**, four flowers are for graves. Red roses are often considered a lover's gift, and avoid chrysanthemums in **France** and **Spain**, where they're associated with funerals.

your place is lovely!

Cz	máš fakt pěknej byt! *mash fakt* **pyek**-ney beet!
Dan	hyggeligt sted, du har! *hue-***guh**-leet stehTH, doo haar!
Dut	je hebt een leuk huis! *ye hehbt en leuk heuis!*
Fr	c'est joli chez toi ! *say jo-lee shay twa!*

Ger	du hast es sehr schön hier! *doo hast ess zehr sheun heer!*
Gr	το σπίτι σου είναι πολύ ωραίο! *to spi-ti soo i-ne po-li o-re-o!*
It	hai una bellissima casa! *ah-ee oo-na bel-lees-see-ma kah-za!*
Por	tem uma casa muito bonita! *taim oo-mUH kah-zUH mooy-too boo-nee-tUH!*
Sp	¡tienes una casa preciosa! *tyen-es oo-na ka-sa preth-yoh-sa!*
Swe	vilket fint ställe du har! *vil-ket feent stel-eh doo hahr!*

shall we put some music on?

Cz	nepustíme nějakou muziku? *ne-poost-eem-e nye-yak-o-oo mooz-eek-oo?*
Dan	skal vi ikke sætte noget musik på? *skal vee ik-kuh seht-tuh no-wuht mu-seek paw?*
Dut	zullen we muziek aanzetten? *zel-e(n) ve moo-zeek ahn-zeht-e(n)?*
Fr	on met de la musique ? *ON may duh la mU-zeek?*
Ger	wollen wir etwas Musik hören? *vol-uhn veer et-vas moo-zeek heur-uhn?*
Gr	να βαλούμε λίγη μουσική; *na va-loo-me li-ghi moo-si-ki?*
It	mettiamo un po' di musica? *met-tee-ah-moh oon poh dee moo-zee-ka?*
Por	que tal um pouco de música? *kae tahl oom po-koo dae moo-zee-kUH?*
Sp	¿ponemos música? *pon-ay-mos moo-see-ka?*
Swe	ska vi lägga på musik? *ska vee legg-a paw moo-seek?*

this is a great party!

Cz	tohle je skvělá party! *to-hle ye skvyel-a par-tee!*
Dan	det er en rigtig god fest! *deh ehr ehn rehk-tee goh fest!*
Dut	dit is een geweldig feest! *dit is en CHe-veld-eCH fayst!*
Fr	cette fête est géniale ! *set fet ay zhay-nyal!*
Ger	das ist eine tolle Party! *das ist ey-nuh tol-uh par-ty!*
Gr	πολύ ωραίο πάρτυ! *po-li o-re-o par-ti!*
It	è una bellissima festa! *ay oo-na bel-lees-see-ma fes-ta!*

Por	grande festa! *gran-d **fehsh**-tUH!*
Sp	qué bien está esta fiesta! *kay byen es-**ta** es-ta **fyes**-ta!*
Swe	det här är en härlig fest! *det hair air en **hair**-lig fest!*

Fun fact!

The **Danish** word **hyggelig** (pronounced *hue-**guh**-leet*) and the **German gemütlich** (*guh-**muut**-liCH*) are adjectives used to describe the cosy atmosphere of getting together with friends to eat, drink and relax. They have no real English equivalent, but are often translated as 'cheerful', 'friendly' or 'cosy'.

Let Me Entertain You

this party's rubbish, let's get out of here!

Cz	tahle party je na prd, pojďme pryč! *ta-hle **par**-tee ye **na** prd, **poydy**-me preech!*
Dan	den her fest er noget lort, lad os smutte! *dehn hehr fest ehr no-wuht loert, lah oss **smuet**-uh!*
Dut	dit feest is saai, laten we gaan! *dit fayst is seye, **laht**-e(n) ve CHahn!*
Fr	cette fête est nulle, allez, on s'en va ! *set fet ay nUl, a-lay, ON sON va!*
Ger	die Party ist ziemlich mies, lass uns abhauen! *dee **par**-ty ist **tseem**-liCH mees, las uns **ab**-how-uhn!*

Gr	πολύ άσχημο πάρτυ, πάμε να φύγουμε! *po-**li** **as**-hi-mo **par**-ti, pa-me na **fi**-ghoo-me!*
It	questa festa fa schifo, andiamocene! *kwes-ta **fes**-ta fa skee-foh, an-dee-**ah**-moh-chay-nay!*
Por	esta festa é uma porcaria, vamos embora! *ehsh-tUH **fehsh**-tUH eh oo-mUH poor-**kUH**-ree-ya, **vUH**-moosh aim-**boh**-rUH!*
Sp	esta fiesta es una porquería, vámonos de aquí! *es-ta **fyes**-ta es oo-na por-kair-**ee**-a, ba-moh-nos day a-**kee**!*
Swe	den här festen är dötrist, vi kan väl smita härifrån! *den hair **fest**-en air **dur**-trist, vee kan vel **smee**-ta **hair**-i-frawn!*

thank you for having me

Cz	děkuju ti za pozvání *dyek-oo-yoo **za** poz-**van**-ee*
Dan	tak, fordi jeg måtte komme *tahk, for-dee yai mawt-tuh **kom**-muh*
Dut	bedankt voor de uitnodiging *be-**dankt** for de euit-nohd-eCH-ing*
Fr	merci de m'avoir invité *mair-see duh ma-vwar AN-vee-tay*
Ger	danke für die Einladung *dang-kuh fuur dee **eyn**-lah-dung*
Gr	σ'ευχαριστώ για την πρόσκληση *sef-ha-ri-**sto** ya tin pro-skli-si*
It	grazie per avermi invitato *grat-see-ay per a-**vair**-mee een-vee-tah-toh*
Por	obrigado *(m)*/obrigada *(f)* pelo convite *oh-bree-**gah**-doo/oh-bree-**gah**-dUH pae-loo kon-**vee**-t*
Sp	gracias por invitarme *grath-yas por een-bee-**tar**-may*
Swe	tack för att jag fick komma *tak fur att yahg fik **komm**-a*

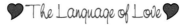

would you like to come in for coffee?

Cz nechceš jít dál na kafe?
nekh-tsesh yeet dal na kaf-e?

Dan har du lyst til at komme ind og få kaffe?
*haar doo luest til att **kom**-muh in oe faw **kah**-fuh?*

156

Dut heb je zin in een kopje koffie?
hehp ye zin in en **kop**-*ye* **kof**-*ee?*

Fr est-ce que tu veux venir prendre le café ?
ess-kuh tU vuh vuh-neer prONdr luh ka-fay?

Ger kann ich dir eine Tasse Kaffee bei mir anbieten?
kan ish deer **ey**-*nuh* **tas**-*uh* **ka**-*fay bey meer* **an**-*bee-tuhn?*

Gr θάθελες να'ρθεις μέσα για ένα καφέ;
THa-*THe-les* **nar**-*THis* **me**-*sa ya* **e**-*na ka*-**fe**?

It ti va di entrare per un caffè?
*tee va dee en-***trah**-*ray per oon kaf-***fay**?

Por quer entrar para tomar um café?
*kehr ain-***trahr** p**UH**-*rUH too-***mahr** *oom k**UH**-**feh**?

Sp ¿entras a tomarte un café?
*en-tras a toh-***mar**-*tay oon ka-***fay**?

Swe skulle du vilja komma in på kaffe?
skool-eh doo **vil**-*ya* **komm**-*a in paw* **kaff**-*eh?*

157

Take Care!

Vital vocab

doctor

Cz	doktor *dok*-tor, lékař *l<u>e</u>k*-arzh
Dan	læge *leh*-juh
Dut	dokter *dok*-ter
Fr	médecin *med-sAN*
Ger	Arzt *ahrtst*
Gr	γιατρός *ya-***tros**
It	medico *may*-dee-koh
Por	médico *mehd*-ee-koo
Sp	médico *med*-ee-koh
Swe	läkare *lair*-ka-reh

chemist's

Cz	lékárna *l<u>e</u>k-<u>a</u>r-na*
Dan	apotek *a-poh-***tehk**
Dut	apotheek *a-poh-***tayk**
Fr	pharmacie *far-ma-see*
Ger	Apotheke *a-poh-***tay**-kuh
Gr	φαρμακείο *far-ma-***ki**-o
It	farmacia *far-ma-***chee**-a
Por	farmácia *fUHr-***ma**-see-UH
Sp	farmacia *far-***math**-ee-a
Swe	apotek *a-po-***tehk**

emergency

Cz	pohotovost	*po-ho-to-vost*
Dan	nødsituation	*noeTH-situ-a-si-on*
Dut	noodgeval	*noht-ge-val*
Fr	urgence	*Ur-zhONs*
Ger	Notfall	*noht-fal*
Gr	επείγον	*e-pi-ghon*
It	emergenza	*ay-mer-gent-sa*
Por	emergência	*ee-mUHr-jaen-see-yUH*
Sp	urgencia	*oor-CHen-thee-a*
Swe	nödsituation	*nurd-sit-oo-a-shoon*

ambulance

Cz	sanitka	*san-eet-ka*
Dan	ambulance	*am-boo-laang-suh*
Dut	ambulance	*am-boo-lans-e*
Fr	ambulance	*ON-bU-lONs*
Ger	Krankenwagen	*krang-kuhn-vah-guhn*
Gr	ασθενοφόρο	*as-THe-no-fo-ro*
It	ambulanza	*am-boo-lant-sa*
Por	ambulância	*UHm-boo-lUHn-see-ya*
Sp	ambulancia	*am-boo-lan-thee-a*
Swe	ambulans	*am-boo-lans*

police

Cz	policie	*po-leet-see-ye*
Dan	politi	*po-le-tee*
Dut	politie	*pohl-i(t)-see*
Fr	police	*po-lees*
Ger	Polizei	*pol-it-sey*
Gr	αστυνομία	*as-ti-no-mi-a*
It	polizia	*po-leet-see-a*
Por	polícia	*poo-lee-see-ya*
Sp	policía	*po-lee-thee-a*
Swe	polis	*po-lees*

fire brigade

Cz	hasiči	*ha-see-chee*
Dan	brandvæsen	*braan-ve-suhn*
Dut	brandweer	*brant-vayr*
Fr	pompiers	*pON-pyay*
Ger	Feuerwehr	*foy-uh-vehr*
Gr	πυροσβεστική	*pi-roz-ves-ti-ki*
It	pompieri	*pom-pee-ay-ree*
Por	bombeiros	*bom-bay-roosh*
Sp	bomberos	*bom-bair-ohs*
Swe	brandkår	*brand-kaw*

Take Care!

In the Know

Although individual countries may have their own emergency numbers, **112** is now the official EU-wide number that will get you whichever service you require. Get a European Health Insurance Card (EHIC) before you travel, which entitles you to free or lower-cost medical treatment in EU countries (you should take out travel health insurance too as not everything is covered by the EHIC). Pharmacies are generally open similar hours to the local shops (sometimes reduced hours at weekends). There will always be a local duty pharmacy open nights and weekends: details are usually displayed in the window of the ordinary chemists, or ask at your accommodation or tourist office. Chemists provide all the usual basic remedies and can usually advise on minor ailments; in some countries (such as Greece and Portugal) you can buy stronger medicines like antibiotics over the counter without prescription.

Condoms are widely available from chemists and supermarkets or from machines in bar and club toilets (and in the street in some countries); they are also sometimes handed out free in clubs (but don't rely on this being the case!). You should take your contraceptive pills with you. The morning-after pill is technically available everywhere, but access to it varies: for example, in France, Italy and Sweden you can buy it over the counter, in Germany you need a prescription and in Spain it's only available from a doctor (for a fee).

When going out in European cities you should take the same precautions you would at home: hang on to your valuables (watch out for pickpockets, especially on public transport, and don't leave bags, phones etc unattended in bars and restaurants) and avoid walking around alone at night, particularly if you're woman.

Drink-driving is illegal all over Europe and laws have been tightened up recently (in the Czech Republic even one drink is breaking the law). However, in some places the message hasn't quite sunk in yet and people may still take their cars on a night out – so be wary about accepting lifts from local friends at night. And don't be tempted to drink and drive yourself as penalties can be harsh. If you're the designated driver, always carry your licence, insurance documents and some other ID. In most cities, public transport runs until around midnight or 1 am. After that, your best bet is usually to get a taxi – check out where the nearest taxi rank is, as it's easier and safer to get a cab there than trying to flag one down. Some cities have nightbus services: bus and train stations, bus stops and tourist offices should have details.

The Netherlands is known for its liberal attitude to drugs, and you can buy and smoke small quantities of cannabis in the famous **coffeeshops**. If you're tempted to indulge, stick to these outlets and don't attempt to bring home any 'souvenirs'! Other drugs are illegal everywhere and it's safest to steer clear.

Over to you

where's the nearest chemists/duty pharmacy?

Cz   kde je (tu) nejbližší lékárna/lékárna s nočním provozem? *kde ye too **ney**-bleezh-shee **lek**-ar-na/**lek**-ar-na s **noch**-neem **prov**-oz-em?*

Dan	hvor er det nærmeste apotek? *vor ehr deh **nehr**-muh-stuh a-poh-**tehk**?*
Dut	waar is de dichtsbijzijnde apotheek? *vahr is de diCHt-**bay**-zayn-de ap-oh-**tayk**?*
Fr	où est la pharmacie/pharmacie de garde la plus proche ? *oo ay la far-ma-**see**/far-ma-see duh gard la plU prosh?*
Ger	wo ist hier die nächste Apotheke? *voh ist heer dee **neCH**-stuh a-poh-**tay**-kuh?*
Gr	πού είναι το κοντινότερο φαρμακείο/εφημερεύον φαρμακείο; *poo i-ne to kon-di-**no**-te-ro far-ma-**ki**-o/e-fi-me-**re**-von far-ma-**ki**-o?*
It	dov'è la farmacia/la farmacia di turno più vicina? *doh-**vay** la far-ma-**chee**-a/la far-ma-**chee**-a dee **toor**-noh pyoo vee-**chee**-na?*
Por	onde é a farmácia mais perto/de serviço? *ond eh UH fUHr-mah-see-yUH mah-eesh **pehr**-too/dae saer-**vee**-soo?*
Sp	¿hay una farmacia/una farmacia de guardia por aquí cerca? *eye **oo**-na far-**math**-ee-a/oo-na far-**math**-ee-a day **gwar**-dee-a por a-**kee** **thair**-ka?*
Swe	var ligger närmaste apotek/jourapotek? *vahr **ligg**-er **nair**-mas-teh a-po-**tehk**/yoor-a-po-**tehk**?*

I need some aspirin/plasters/something for an upset stomach

Cz	potřebuju aspirín/náplasti/něco na žaludeční nevolnost *pot-rzhe-boo-yoo **asp**-ee-**reen**/**nap**-last-ee/**nyet**-so na zhal-oo-dech-**nee** ne-vol-nost*
Dan	jeg har brug for nogle hovedpinepiller/noget plaster/noget for dårlig mave *yai haar broo for **no**-luh hoe**TH**-peen-pil-luhr/**no**-wuht **plas**-tuhr/**no**-wuht for **dawr**-lee **ma**-wuh*
Dut	ik heb asperine/pleisters/iets nodig, want mijn maag is van streek *ik hehp as-per-**in**-e/**playst**-ers/eets **nohd**-eCH, vant mayn mahCH is van strayk*
Fr	j'ai besoin d'aspirine/de pansements/de quelque chose contre les indigestions *zhay buh-zwAN das-pee-reen/duh pON-suh-mON/duh kel-kuh shohz kontr layz AN-dee-zhes-tyON*

162

Ger ich brauche Aspirin/Pflaster/etwas gegen Magenschmerzen
*ish brow-CHuh as-pee-reen/pflas-tuh/et-vas gay-gun mah-guhn-
shmert-suhn*

Gr χρειάζομαι απιρίνες/χανζαπλάστ/κάτι για το στομάχι *hri-a-zo-
me a-spi-ri-nes/han-za-plast/ka-ti ya to sto-ma-hi*

It ho bisogno di aspirine/di cerotti/di qualcosa per il mal di
stomaco *oh bee-zon-yoh dee as-pee-ree-nay/dee cher-ot-tee/dee
kwal-koh-za per eel mal dee sto-ma-koh*

Por queria aspirinas/pensos rápidos/alguma coisa para o estô-
mago *ke-ree-UH ash-pee-ree-nUHsh/pain-soosh RRah-pee-doosh/
al-goo-mUH koy-zUH pUH-rUH oo esh-toh-mUH-goo*

Sp necesito aspirinas/tiritas/algo para el dolor de estómago *ne-
thay-see-toh as-pee-ree-nas/tee-ree-tas/al-goh pa-ra el do-lor day
es-tom-a-goh*

Swe jag behöver aspirin/plåster/någonting för en dålig mage *yahg
be-hur-ver as-pi-reen/plaw-ster/naw-gon-ting fur en daw-lig mahg-
eh*

do you have any condoms?

Cz máš kondomy? *mash kon-dom-ee?*

Dan har du nogen kondomer? *haar doo no-wuhn kon-doh-muhr?*

Dut heb je condooms? *hehp ye kon-dohms?*

Fr est-ce que tu as des préservatifs ? *ess kuh tU a day pray-zair-
va-teef?*

Ger hast du Kondome? *hast doo kon-doh-muh?*

Gr έχεις προφυλακτικά; *e-his pro-fi-la-kti-ka?*

It hai dei preservativi? *ah-ee day-ee pray-zer-va-tee-vee?*

Por tem preservativos? *taim prae-zaer-vUH-tee-voosh?*

Sp ¿tienes condones? *tyen-es kon-doh-nays?*

Swe har du kondomer? *har doo kon-doo-mer?*

Fun fact!

You may have noticed that in several languages the word for 'condom' looks a bit like 'preservative' – to avoid confusion, think of it as something to preserve your health rather than anything to do with food!

I need the morning-after pill

Cz	potřebuji postinor *po-trzh-e-boo-yee **pos**-tee-nor*
Dan	jeg har brug for en fortrydelsespille *yai haar broo for ehn for-**trueTH**-uhl-suhs-pill-uh*
Dut	ik heb de morning-afterpil nodig *ik hehp de **mor**-ning **af**-ter-pil **nohd**-eCH*
Fr	j'ai besoin de la pilule du lendemain *zhay buh-zwAN duh la pee-lUl dU lON-duh-mAN*
Ger	ich hätte gerne die Pille danach *ish **het**-uh **gehr**-nuh dee **pil**-uh da-**naCH***
Gr	χρειάζομαι το χάπι της επόμενης μέρας *hri-**a**-zo-me to **ha**-pi tis e-**po**-me-nis **me**-ras*
It	ho bisogno della pillola del giorno dopo *oh bee-**zon**-yoh **del**-la **peel**-loh-la del **jor**-noh **do**-poh*
Por	preciso da pílula do dia seguinte *prae-**see**-zoo dUH **pee**-loo-lUH doo **dee**-ya sae-**geen**-t*

Sp necesito la píldora del día después *ne-thay-**see**-toh la **peel**-dor-a del **dee**-a des-**pwes***

Swe jag behöver ta dagen efter-p-piller *yahg be-**hur**-ver tah **dahg**-en ef-ter-pee-**pill**-er*

I've got a hangover

Cz mám kocovinu *m*ạ*m **kots**-ov-een-oo*

Dan jeg har tømmermænd *yai haar **toem**-muhr-mehn*

Dut ik heb een kater *ik hehp en **kah**-ter*

Fr j'ai la gueule de bois *zhay la guhl duh bwa*

Ger ich habe voll 'nen Kater *ish **hah**-buh fol nuhn **kah**-tuh*

Gr έχω πονοκέφαλο από ποτό/χανγκόβερ *e-ho po-no-**ke**-fa-lo a-**po** po-**to**/han-**go**-ver*

It mi sto rimettendo da una sbornia *mee stoh ree-met-**ten**-do da oo-na **zbor**-nee-a*

Por estou de ressaca *esh-tow dae RRae-**sah**-kUH*

Sp tengo resaca *teng-goh ray-**sa**-ka*

Swe jag har baksmälla *yahg hahr bahks-**mell**-a*

Fun facts!

The **French** word for a hangover, **la gueule de bois**, literally means 'the mouth made of wood' – quite an appropriate image! In **Germany** it's known as **ein Kater** (literally 'a tomcat', and the traditional cure is a nice plate of rollmops (pickled herrings).

I think I've got food poisoning

Cz myslím, že mám otravu ze zkaženého jídla *mees-leem, zhe mam ot-rav-oo ze zka-zhen-e-ho yeed-la*

Dan jeg tror, jeg har fået maveforgiftning *yai troer, yai haar faw-uht ma-wuh-for-geeft-ning*

Dut ik denk dat ik voedselvergiftiging heb *ik dehnk dat ik foods-el-ver-CHift-e-ging hehp*

Fr je crois que j'ai une intoxication alimentaire *zhuh krwa kuh zhay Un AN-tok-see-ka-syON al-ee-mON-tair*

Ger ich glaube ich habe eine Lebensmittelvergiftung *ish glow-buh ish hah-buh ey-nuh lay-buhnz-mit-uhl-fehr-gif-tung*

Gr νομίζω ότι έχω πάθει δηλητηρίαση *no-mi-zo o-ti e-ho pa-THi thi-li-ti-ri-a-si*

It credo di avere un'intossicazione alimentare *kray-doh dee a-vay-ray oon-een-tos-see-kat-see-oh-nay a-lee-men-tah-ray*

Por acho que apanhei uma intoxicação alimentar *ah-shoo kae UH-pUHn-yay oo-mUH een-tohk-shee-kUH-souŋ UH-lee-main-tahr*

Sp creo que tengo una intoxicación alimentaria *kray-oh kay teng-goh oo-na een-tok-see-kath-yohn a-lee-men-tar-ee-a*

Swe jag tror jag har fått matförgiftning *yahg tror yahg har fott maht-fur-yift-ning*

does anyone here speak English?

Cz mluví tady někdo anglicky? *mloo-vee tad-ee nyek-do an-gleets-kee?*

Dan er der nogen her, der taler engelsk? *ehr dehr no-wuhn hehr, dehr tal-uhr eng-uhlsk?*

Dut spreekt iemand hier Engels? *spraykt ee-mant heer ehng-els?*

Fr est-ce-que quelqu'un parle anglais ? *ess kuh kel-kAN parl ON-glay?*

Ger spricht irgendjemand hier Englisch? *shprisht eer-guhnt-yay-mand heer eng-lish?*

Gr υπάρχει κανείς εδώ που να μιλάει αγγλικά; *i-par-hi ka-nis e-tho poo na mi-la-i an-gli-ka?*

It   c'è qualcuno qui che parla inglese? *chay kwal-**koo**-noh kwee kay par-la eeng-**glay**-zay?*

Por   alguém fala inglês? *al-**gaim** fah-lUH een-**glaysh**?*

Sp   ¿habla alguien inglés? *ab-la **al**-gyen eeng-**glays**?*

Swe   finns det någon här som pratar engelska? *finns det **naw**-gon hair som **praht**-er **eng**-el-ska?*

could I borrow your phone, please?

Cz   prosím vás, můžu si vypůjčit váš telefon? *pro-<u>seem</u> v<u>a</u>s, **moozh**-oo see vee-<u>pooy</u>-cheet v<u>a</u>sh **te**-le-fon?*

Dan   må jeg låne din telefon? *maw yai **law**-nuh deen te-luh-**fon**?*

Dut   zou ik uw telefoon mogen lenen, alstublieft? *zow ik oo tay-le-foon moh-CHe(n) **lay**-ne(n), als-too-**bleeft**?*

Fr   est-ce que je pourrais utiliser votre téléphone, s'il vous plaît ? *ess kuh zhuh poo-ray U-tee-lee-zay votr tel-ay-fon, seel voo play?*

Ger   darf ich mal telefonieren bitte? *darf ish mahl te-lay-foh-**neer**-uhn bit-uh?*

Gr   θα μπορούσα να δανειστώ το τηλέφωνό σας, παρακαλώ; *THa bo-**roo**-sa na tha-ni-**sto** to ti-**le**-fo-**no** sas, pa-ra-ka-**lo**?*

It   mi può prestare il suo telefono, per favore? *mee pwo pres-**tah**-ray eel **soo**-oh tay-**lef**-o-noh, per fa-**vor**-ay?*

Por   posso utilizar o seu telefone, se faz favor? *poh-soo oo-tee-lee-**zahr** oo **say**-oo te-le-**foh**-n, s-**fahsh** fUH-**vor**?*

Sp   ¿puedo usar su teléfono? *pway-doh oo-**sar** soo tel-**ay**-fon-oh?*

Swe   kan jag låna din telefon? *kan yahg **lawn**-a din te-le-**foon**?*

my bag/wallet's been stolen

Cz   ukradli mi tašku (*bag*)/kabelku (*handbag*)/peněženku *oo-krad-lee mee **tash**-koo/**kab**-el-koo/**pen**-yezh-en-koo*

Dan   min taske/pung er blevet stjålet *meen **tas**-kuh/puhng ehr **ble**-wuht **stjaw**-luht*

Dut   mijn tas/portemonnee is gestolen *mayn tas/por-te-mon-**ay** is CHe-**stoh**-le(n)*

167

Fr	on m'a volé mon sac/mon portefeuille *ON ma vo-lay mON sak/mON por-tuh-foy*
Ger	meine Tasche/mein Portemonee wurde gestohlen *mey-nuh ta-shuh/meyn port-mon-ay voor-duh guh-shtoh-luhn*
Gr	μου έκλεψαν την τσάντα μου/το πορτοφόλι μου *moo e-kle-psan tin tsan-da moo/to por-to-fo-li moo*
It	mi hanno rubato la borsa/il portafogli *mee an-noh roo-bah-toh la bor-sa/eel por-ta-fo-lyee*
Por	roubaram-me a carteira *RRo-bah-rouŋ-mae UH kUHr-tay-rUH*
Sp	me han robado el bolso/la cartera *may han ro-bah-doh el bol-soh/la kar-tair-a*
Swe	min väska/plånbok har blivit stulen *min ves-ka/plawn-book hahr blee-vit stoo-len*

I've been attacked

Cz	napadli mě *na-pad-lee mnye*
Dan	jeg er blevet overfaldet *yai ehr ble-wuht ow-er-fallt*
Dut	ik ben aangevallen *ik behn ahn-CHe-fal-e(n)*
Fr	j'ai été agressé *zhay et-ay a-gress-ay*
Ger	ich bin überfallen worden *ish bin uu-ber-fal-uhn vor-duhn*
Gr	μου επιτέθηκαν *moo e-pi-te-THi-kan*
It	sono stato aggredito (m)/aggredita (f) *son-oh stah-toh ag-gray-dee-toh/ag-gray-dee-tah*
Por	fui atacado (m)/atacada (f) *fooy-ee UH-tUH-kah-doo/UH-tUH-kah-dUH*
Sp	he sufrido una agresión *ay soo-free-doh oo-na a-gres-yohn*
Swe	jag har blivit överfallen *yahg har blee-vit ur-ver-fall-en*

there's a man following me

Cz	nějaký muž mě sleduje *nye-yak-ee moozh mnye sled-oo-ye*
Dan	der er en mand, der følger efter mig *der ehr ehn man, der feul-yuhr eft-uhr mai*
Dut	een man achtervolgt mij *en man aCHt-er-volCHt may*
Fr	il y a un homme qui me suit *eel ya AN om kee mUH swee*

168

Ger	ein Mann verfolgt mich *eyn man fehr-folgt mish*
Gr	με ακολουθεί ένας άντρας *me a-ko-loo-THi e-nas an-dras*
It	c'è un uomo che mi segue *chay oon oo-oh-moh kay mee say-gway*
Por	um homem anda a seguir-me *oom oh-maim UHn-dUH UH sae-geer-mae*
Sp	un hombre me está siguiendo *oon om-bray may es-ta see-gyen-doh*
Swe	en man följer efter mig *en man ful-yer ef-ter may*

there's been an accident

Cz	stala se nehoda *sta-la se ne-hod-a*
Dan	der er sket en ulykke *dehr ehr skeht ehn u-loek-kuh*
Dut	er is een ongeluk gebeurt *ehr is en on-CHe-lek CHe-beurt*
Fr	il y a eu un accident *eel ya U AN ak-see-dON*
Ger	es ist ein Unfall passiert *ess ist eyn un-fal pas-eert*
Gr	έγινε ένα ατύχημα *e-ghi-ne e-na a-ti-hi-ma*
It	c'è stato un incidente *chay sta-toh oon een-chee-den-tay*
Por	houve um acidente *oh-v oom UH-see-dain-t*
Sp	ha habido un accidente *a a-bee-doh oon ak-thee-den-tay*
Swe	det har hänt en olycka *det har hent en oo-luk-a*

where's the nearest police station/hospital?

Cz	kde je (tu) nejbližší policejní stanice/nemocnice? *kde ye (too) ney-bleezh-shee pol-eets-ey-nee stan-ee-tse/ne-mots-nee-tse?*
Dan	hvor er den nærmeste politistation/det nærmeste hospital? *vor ehr dehn nehr-muh-stuh po-le-tee-sta-si-on/deh nehr-muh-stuh hos-pi-tal?*
Dut	waar is het dichtsbijzijnde politiebureau/ziekenhuis? *vahr is het diCHt-bay-zayn-de pohl-i(t)-see-boor-oh/zeek-e(n)-heuis*
Fr	où est le commissariat le plus proche/l'hôpital le plus proche? *oo ay le kom-ee-sar-ee-a luh plU prosh/lop-ee-tal luh plU prosh?*
Ger	wo ist das nächste Polizeirevier/Krankenhaus? *voh ist das neCH-stuh pol-it-sey-ruh-veer/krang-kuhn-hows?*

169

Gr	πού είναι το κοντινότερο αστυνομικό τμήμα/νοσοκομείο; *poo i-ne to kon-di-**no**-te-ro a-sti-no-mi-**ko** t**mi**-ma/no-so-ko-**mi**-o?*
It	dov'è il commissariato/l'ospedale più vicino? *doh-**vay** eel kom-mees-sa-ree-**ah**-toh/los-pay-**dah**-lay pyoo vee-**chee**-noh?*
Por	onde é a esquadra de polícia mais próxima/o hospital mais próximo? *ond eh UH esh-**kwah**-drUH dae poo-**lee**-see-ya **mah**-eesh **proh**-see-mUH/oo ohsh-pee-**tahl mah**-eesh **proh**-see-moo?*
Sp	¿dónde está la comisaría más cercana/el hospital más cercano? *don-day es-**ta** la kom-ee-sa-**ree**-a mas thair-**kah**-na/el os-pee-**tahl** mas thair-**kah**-noh?*
Swe	var ligger närmaste polisstation/sjukhus? *vahr **ligg**-er nair-**mas**-teh po-**lees**-sta-**shoon**/**shook**-hoos?*

call the police/an ambulance!

Cz	zavolejte policii/sanitku! *za-vol-ey-te **pol**-eets-ee-ee/**san**-eet-koo!*
Dan	tilkald politiet/en ambulance! *til-kall po-le-**tee**-uht/ehn am-boo-**laang**-suh!*
Dut	bel de politie/ambulance! *behl de pohl-**i**(t)-see/am-boo-**lan**-se!*
Fr	appelez la police/une ambulance ! *a-puh-lay la po-lees/Un ON-bU-lONs!*
Ger	ruf die Polizei/einen Krankenwagen! *roof dee pol-it-**sey**/**eyn**-uhn **krang**-kuhn-vah-guhn!*
Gr	καλέστε την αστυνομία/ένα ασθενοφόρο! *ka-**le**-ste tin a-sti-no-**mi**-a/**e**-na as-THe-no-**fo**-ro!*
It	chiamate la polizia/un'ambulanza! *kee-a-**mah**-tay la po-leet-**see**-a/oon-am-boo-**lant**-sa!*
Por	chamem a polícia/uma ambulância! *shUH-maim UH poo-**lee**-see-ya/**oo**-mUH UHm-boo-**lan**-see-ya!*
Sp	¡llame a la policía/a una ambulancia! *yah-may a la po-lee-**thee**-a/a **oo**-na am-boo-**lan**-thee-a!*
Swe	ring polisen/efter en ambulans! *ring po-**lees**-en/**ef**-ter en am-boo-**lans**!*

help!

Cz	pomoc! *po-mots!*	
Dan	hjælp! *yehlp!*	
Dut	help! *help!*	
Fr	au secours ! *ohs-koor!*	
Ger	Hilfe! *hil-fuh!*	
Gr	βοήθεια! *vo-i-THi-a!*	
It	aiuto! *a-yoo-toh!*	
Por	socorro! *soo-ko-RRoo!*, ajuda! *UH-Joo-dUH!*	
Sp	¡socorro! *so-koRR-oh!*	
Swe	hjälp! *yelp!*	

he's/she's had too much to drink

Cz vypil/vypila toho hrozně moc *vee-peel/vee-pee-la to-ho hroz-nye mots*

Dan han/hun har fået for meget at drikke *han/hoon haar faw-uht for mai-yuht at dre-kuh*

Dut hij/zij heeft te veel gedronken *hay/zay hayft te fayl CHe-dronk-e(n)*

Fr il/elle a trop bu *eel/ell a tro bU*

Ger er/sie hat zu viel getrunken *ehr/zee hat tsoo feel guh-trung-kuhn*

Gr ήπιε πάρα πολύ *i-pi-e pa-ra po-li*

It ha bevuto troppo *a bay-voo-toh trop-poh*

Por bebeu demais *bae-bay-oo dae-mah-eesh*

Sp ha bebido más de la cuenta *a be-bee-doh mas day la kwen-ta*

Swe han/hon har druckit för mycket *han/hoon hahr droo-kit fur muk-eh*

he's/she's taken ecstasy/cocaine/speed

Cz vzal/vzala si extázi/kokain/speed *vzal/vzal-a syee ek-stas-ee/kok-a-yeen/speed*

Dan han/hun har taget ecstasy/kokain/speed *han/hoon haar ta-yuht eks-ta-see/ko-ka-een/speed*

Dut hij/zij heeft exstasy/cocaïne/speed gebruikt *hay/zay hayft eks-te-see/koh-keye-een-e/speet CHe-breuikt*

Take Care!

171

Fr	il/elle a pris de l'ecstasy/de la cocaïne/du speed *eel/ell a pree duh lek-sta-see/duh la ko-keye-een/dU speed*
Ger	er/sie hat Ecstasy/Kokain/Speed genommen *ehr/zee hat eks-ta-sy/koh-ka-een/speed guh-nom-uhm*
Gr	έχει πάρει έκσταση/κοκαίνη/σπιντ *e-hi pa-ri ek-sta-si/ko-ka-i-ni/spid*
It	ha preso dell'ecstasy/della cocaina/dello speed *a pray-zo del-lek-sta-zee/del-la koh-ka-ee-na/del-lo speed*
Por	tomou ecstasy/cocaína/speed *too-mow ek-stUH-see/koh-kUH-ee-nUH/speed*
Sp	ha tomado éxtasis/cocaína/speed *a to-mah-doh ek-sta-sees/koh-keye-ee-na/speed*
Swe	han/hon har tagit ecstasy/kokain/amfetamin *han/hoon hahr tah-git eks-ta-see/koo-kayn/am-fe-ta-meen*

Fun facts!

Although illegal in most places, smoking dope is not uncommon among young Europeans. Words for the drug include **shit** in **France**, **hash/hasch** in **Denmark** and **Sweden** respectively and **tráva** (grass) in the **Czech Republic**. Names for a joint include **un porro** in **Spain**, **una canna** in **Italy** and **un pétard** or **un joint** (pronounced *zhwAN*) in **France**.

no thanks, I don't do drugs

Cz	ne, děkuju, neberu drogy	*ne, dyek-oo-yoo, ne-ber-oo drog-ee*
Dan	nej tak, jeg tager ikke stoffer	*nai tahk, yai taar ik-kuh stof-fuhr*
Dut	nee dankje, ik gebruik geen drugs	*nay dank ye, ik CHe-breuik CHayn dreCHs*
Fr	non merci, je ne prends pas de drogue	*nON mair-see, zhuh nuh prON pa duh drog*
Ger	nein danke, ich nehme keine Drogen	*neyn dang-kuh, ish nay-muh key-nuh droh-guhn*
Gr	όχι ευχαριστώ, δεν παίρνω ναρκωτικά	*o-hi ef-ha-ri-sto, then per-no nar-ko-ti-ka*
It	no grazie, non prendo droga	*noh grat-see-ay, non pren-doh droh-ga*
Por	não obrigado (m)/obrigada (f), não consumo drogas	*nouŋ oh-bree-gah-doo/oh-bree-gah-dUH, nouŋ kon-soo-moo droh-gUHsh*
Sp	no gracias, no me drogo	*noh grath-yas, noh may droh-goh*
Swe	nej tack, jag använder inte knark	*ney tak, yahg an-ven-der in-teh knark*

leave me alone!

Cz	nechte mě na pokoji!	*nekh-te mnye na pok-oy-ee!*
Dan	lad mig være i fred!	*laTH mai vaeh-ruh ee frehTH!*
Dut	laat me met rust!	*laht me meht rest!*
Fr	laisse-moi tranquille !	*less mwa trON-keel!*
Ger	lass mich in Ruhe!	*lass mish in roo-uh!*
Gr	άσε με ήσυχο/ήσυχη!	*a-se me i-si-ho/i-si-hi!*
It	lasciami in pace!	*lash-a-mee een pah-chay!*
Por	deixe-me em paz!	*daysh-mae aim pahsh!*
Sp	¡déjame en paz!	*de-CHa-may en path!*
Swe	lämna mig ifred!	*lem-na may i-freed!*

stop it or I'll call the police!

Cz	přestaňte/nechte toho, nebo zavolám policii! *przhe-stany-te/ nekh-te to-ho, ne-bo za-vol-am pol-eets-ee-ee!*
Dan	stop eller jeg tilkalder politiet! *stop el-luh yai til-kall-uhr po-le-tee-uht!*
Dut	stop daarmee, anders bel ik de politie! *stop dahr-may, an-ders behl ik de pohl-i(t)-see!*
Fr	arrête, sinon j'appelle la police ! *a-ret, see-nON zha-pel la po-lees!*
Ger	hör sofort auf oder ich rufe die Polizei! *heur zoh-fort owf oh-duh ish roo-fuh dee pol-it-sey!*
Gr	σταμάτα γιατί θα καλέσω την αστυνομία! *sta-ma-ta ya-ti THa ka-le-so tin a-sti-no-mi-a!*
It	smettila o chiamo la polizia! *zmet-tee-la oh kee-ah-moh la po-leet-see-a!*
Por	pare ou chamo a polícia! *pahr o shUH-moo UH poo-lee-see-ya!*
Sp	para o llamo a la policía! *pa-ra oh yah-moh a la po-lee-thee-a!*
Swe	sluta eller så ringer jag polisen! *sloo-ta ell-er saw ring-er yahg po-lees-en!*

💛 The Language of Love 💛

did you hurt yourself when you fell from heaven?

Cz co tady dělá taková božská bytost?
tso tad-ee dyel-a tak-ov-a bozh-ska beet-ost?

Dan slog du dig, da du faldt ned fra himlen?
slo doo dai, da doo falt neTH fra him-luhn?

Dut heb je jezelf pijn gedaan toen je uit de hemel viel?
hehp ye ye-zelf payn CHe-dahn toon ye euit de haym-el feel?

Fr est-ce que tu t'es fait mal en tombant du paradis?
ess kuh tU tay fay mal ON tON-bON dU pa-ra-dee?

174

Ger hast du dir weh getan, als du vom Himmel fielst?
*hast doo deer vay guh-**tahn**, als doo fom **him**-uhl feelst?*

Gr χτύπησες όταν έπεσες από τον ουρανό;
*hti-pi-ses **o**-tan e-pe-ses a-**po** ton oo-ra-**no**?*

It ti sei fatto *(m)*/fatta *(f)* male cadendo dal cielo?
*tee **say**-ee **fat**-toh/**fat**-tah **mah**-lay ka-**den**-doh dal **chay**-loh?*

Por magoou-se quando caiu do céu?
*mUHg-**woh**-sae **kwUHn**-doo kUH-**yoo** doo **seh**-oo?*

Sp ¿te hiciste daño al caer del cielo?
*tay ee-**thees**-tay **dan**-yoh al ka-**air** del **thyay**-loh?*

Swe slog du dig när du föll från himlen?
*sloog doo day nair doo full frawn **him**-len?*